CHALLENGING HISTORY
RESOURCE PACK

BRITAIN 1900–1914
Liz Petheram

Thomas Nelson & Sons Ltd
Nelson House
Mayfield Road
Walton-on-Thames
Surrey KT12 5PL
United Kingdom

First published by Thomas Nelson & Sons Ltd 1999

ISBN: 0-17-435202-6
9 8 7 6 5 4 3 2 1
03 02 01 00 99

Production team
Commissioning and development: Steve Berry
Cover design: Michael Fay
Book design and illustration: Jordan Publishing Design
Editorial: Marie Lister
Photo research: Image Select International

Printed in the UK by Antony Rowe Ltd, Chippenham

Photo acknowledgements
The publishers are grateful to the following for permission to reproduce photographs: The Hulton Getty Picture Collection Limited: p13; Illustrated London News: cover, p12 (Keir Hardie, Ramsay MacDonald), Image Select: p12 (top).

Contents

Sources

Adelman *The Rise of the Labour Party 1880–1945* (1972) Longman

Amery, L.S. *My Political Life* (1953) Hutchinson

Asquith, H.H. Speech to the House of Commons 2 December 1909 in *Hansard Parliamentary Debates*, 5th series, vol. 13, col. 557–8

Balfour, Earl of, *Opinions and Arguments from Speeches and Addresses of the Earl of Balfour* (1927) Hodder and Stoughton

Benning, K. *Edwardian Britain* (1980) Blackie

Bernstein, G.L. *Liberalism and Liberal Politics in Edwardian England* (1986) George Allen

Bonham-Carter, Lady Violet *Winston Churchill as I Knew Him* (1965) Eyre and Spottiswoode

Booth, William *In Darkest England and the Way Out* (1890) Knight's edition (1970)

Bruce, M. *The Coming of the Welfare State* (1961) Batsford

Butler and Jones (eds) *Britain in the 20th Century Documentary Reader* (1994) Heinemann

Childers, Erskine *The Riddle of the Sands* (1903) Sidgwick & Jackson (1978)

Chiozza, L.G. *Money, Riches and Poverty* (1905) Methuen & Co

Churchill, W.S. 'The Untrodden Field of Politics' *The Nation* 7 March 1908

Clarke, P.F. *Lancashire and the New Liberalism* (1971) Cambridge University Press

Dangerfield, G. *The Strange Death of Liberal England* (1936) Constable

Fraser *Evolution of the Welfare State* (1973) Macmillan

Gibbs, Sir Philip *The Pageant of the Years* (1946) Heinemann

Grey, Sir Edward, memo on Franco-German tension in Morocco, 20 February 1906 in G.P. Gooch and H. Temperley (eds) *British Documents on the Origins of War 1898–1914 vol III: the Testing of the Entente, 1904–1906* (1928) HMSO

Hare, J., Boughton, J. and Vinson, A. 'The Transformation of the Two-party System' in *From Liberalism to Labour 1900–1924*, HiDES

HiDES: http://www.psmedia.com/hides.htm

Hopkin *Social History of the English Working Classes* (1979) Hodder and Stoughton

Howarth, T. *20th Century History: The World Since 1900* (1979) Longman

Lansdowne, Speech to the House of Lords in November 1909 in *Hansard Parliamentary Debates*, 5th series, vol. IV. col. 731–50

Lloyd George, Speech to the House of Commons 29 April 1909 in *Hansard Parliamentary Debates*, 5th series, vol. IV, col. 548

Morgan, K.O. *The Age of Lloyd George, the Liberal Party and British Politics 1890–1929* (1971) Allen and Unwin

Morley, Ann and Stanley, Liz *The Life and Death of Emily Wilding Davison* (1988) The Women's Press

Pankhurst, Emmiline *My Own Story* (1914) Virago edition (1979)

Pearce and Stewart *British Political History 1867–1990* (1992) Routledge

Pelling, H. 'Labour and the Downfall of Liberalism' in *Popular Politics and Society in Late Victorian Britain* (1968) Macmillan

Pelling and Reid *A Short History of the Labour Party* (1961) Macmillan

Philips, G. *The Rise of the Labour Party* (1992) Routledge

Pollard *The Development of the British Economy 1914–15* (1963) Edward Arnold

Pugh, M. *The Making of Modern British Politics* (1982) Blackwell Publishers

Pugh, Martin *Women's Suffrage in Britain 1867–1928* (1980) The Historical Association

Read, D. *Documents from Edwardian England* (1973) Harrap

Redmond, Speech to the House of Commons 1912 in *Hansard Parliamentary Debates*, 5th series, vol. xxxvi, col. 1424–6

Reekes, A. *The Rise of Labour 1899–1951* (1991) Macmillan

Rowntree, B.S. *Poverty, a Study in Town Life* (1902) Macmillan

Russell, A.K. *Liberal Landslide: the General Election of 1906* (1973) David and Charles

Samuel, Herbert *Liberalism* (1902) Grant, Richards

Scott, C.P. *C.P. Scott Diaries 1911–28* Trevor Wilson (ed.) (1970) Collins

Snowden, Philip *An Autobiography vol. 1* (1934) Nicolson and Watson

Tanner, D. 'The Rise of the Labour Party' *Modern History Review* November 1989

Traynor, John, *Europe 1890–1990* (1992) Nelson

Webb, Beatrice *Our Partnership* B. Drake and M.I. Cole (eds) (1948) Longman

Webb, Beatrice *Beatrice Webb Diaries 1912–1914* (1952) Longman

Webb, Sidney, 'Lord Rosebery's Escape from Houndsditch' *The Nineteenth Century* vol. 50 September 1901

Wilson, T. *Downfall of the Liberal Party* (1966) Collins and HiDES

1906 GENERAL ELECTION – A LIBERAL LANDSLIDE?

Preview

Conservative governments dominated the last fifteen years of the nineteenth century and were in power up until 1906. The election of that year resulted in a Liberal landslide victory in which they returned 400 seats compared with 157 for the Conservative and Unionist Party. Why was there such a change in Liberal fortune? Was it the nature of the election campaign, the new Liberal policies they had to offer, or was it mainly a huge anti-Tory vote by electors seeking a complete change of government after so many years?

Source A – Election Results

	1900		1906	
	Seats	**% vote**	**Seats**	**% vote**
Cons and Lib.U	402	51.1	157	43.6
Liberal	184	44.6	400	49.0
Labour	2	1.8	30	5.9
Irish Nat.	82	2.5	83	0.6
Others	0	0.0	0	0.9

Election Swing

CONSERVATIVE

219 → Liberal   25 → Labour

Source B

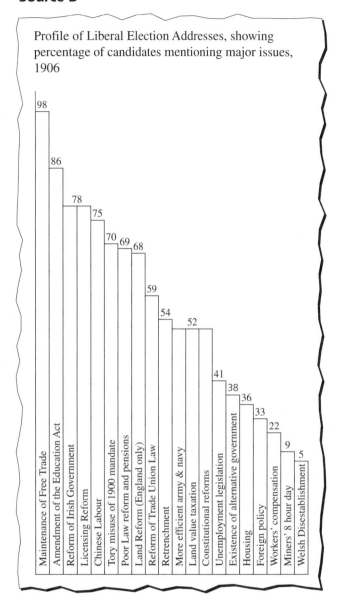

Profile of Liberal Election Addresses, showing percentage of candidates mentioning major issues, 1906

- Maintenance of Free Trade – 98
- Amendment of the Education Act – 86
- Reform of Irish Government – 78
- Licensing Reform – 75
- Chinese Labour – 70
- Tory misuse of 1900 mandate – 69
- Poor Law reform and pensions – 68
- Land Reform (England only) – 59
- Reform of Trade Union Law – 54
- Retrenchment – 52
- More efficient army & navy – 41
- Land value taxation – 38
- Constitutional reforms – 36
- Unemployment legislation – 33
- Existence of alternative government – 22
- Housing – 9
- Foreign policy – 5
- Workers' compensation
- Miners' 8 hour day
- Welsh Disestablishment

From: A.K. Russell, *Liberal Landslide: the General Election of 1906* (1973)

Source C

Number of unopposed returns, Unionist and Liberal, 1885–1906 (England, Scotland, and Wales)

Year	Total no. of seats	Total no. of unopposed returns	No. of Unionist returns unopposed	No. of Liberal returns unopposed (inc. LRC)
1885	567	26	7	19
1886	567	153	114	39
1892	567	51	33	18
1895	567	135	123	12
1900	567	176	153	23
1906	567	37	5	32

From: A.K. Russell, *Liberal Landslide: the General Election of 1906* (1973)

Source D

A candidate had only to be a Free Trader to get in, whether he was known or unknown, semi-Unionist or thorough Home Ruler, Protestant or Roman Catholic, entertaining or dull. He had only to be a Protectionist to lose all chance of getting in though he spoke with the tongues of men and angels, though he was a good employer to many electors, or had led the House of Commons or fought in the Crimea.

Manchester Guardian, 15 January 1906; quoted in Pearce and Stewart's *British Political History 1867–1990* (1992); © *The Guardian*

Source E

Liberal Party, and Conservative and Unionist Party 1906 general election posters
(Geoffrey Ford, private collection)

Questions surrounding the 1906 General Election

How strong was the Liberal Party in 1906?

Was the new Labour Party a threat?

Was this an anti-Tory vote?

How influential was New Liberalism?

TASKS

1 Research further each argument below, possibly find others, and put together a case for and against to be presented for debate.

"It was not the Liberals who won but the Conservatives who lost."

2 Complete an essay in answer to this statement using the structure below as a plan for the analysis. Ensure each paragraph addresses the question in its first sentence and the conclusion is arrived at logically and coherently.

AGREE

1 The contest seems closer than suggested by the number of MPs returned to Parliament when it is noted that Liberals polled 49% of total votes but Conservatives polled 43.6% of total votes. The 'first past the post' system worked heavily in the Liberal Party's favour – a system of proportional representation would have brought a different set of results. WHY?

2 Joseph Chamberlain's proposals for tariff reform divided the government, lost support with the electorate and gave the Liberals an opportunity to unite on the familiar issue of Free Trade. WHY?

3 The 1902 Education Act and 1904 Licensing Act were readily criticised by the Nonconformists and the Temperance Movement. WHY?

4 In South Africa, the Boer War victory had revealed fundamental defence and military problems for which the Conservative government took the blame. WHY?

5 The humanitarian issue of 'Chinese Slavery' in South Africa and the Taff Vale decision at home similarly brought the government under attack. WHY?

6 Conservative Party organisation suffered damage 1903–06 from internal power struggles. Chief Agent Welles proved less capable than his predecessor, and Prime Minister Balfour lacked charisma, rhetoric and the ability to hold a divided and declining party together. WHY?

DISAGREE

1 The Liberal Party went to the polls united behind the traditional issues such as Free Trade, Nonconformity, Temperance, Humanitarianism. Nineteenth-century Liberalism appeared relevant. WHY?

2 Liberals fought the election on a broad range of issues incorporating traditional and progressive attitudes within the party. HOW?

3 A group of younger Liberal candidates were campaigning on a 'New Liberal' ticket promising social reform – old age pensions and Poor Law reform being the most common. New Liberalism offered a political counter to the new Labour Party. HOW?

4 Liberal Party organisation had been greatly improved under Herbert Gladstone. Local associations were rationalised and revitalised, seats were targeted and only five Conservatives stood unopposed in 1906 compared with 153 in 1900. HOW?

5 A secret electoral pact was signed in 1903 between the Liberal Chief Whip, Herbert Gladstone, and the secretary of the Labour Representation Committee, Ramsay MacDonald. It was agreed Labour could contest 30 seats without a Liberal candidate. The Liberals had access to the LRC's £100,000 election fund. Some historians consider it dangerous for the Liberals to have tacitly accepted a party which could replace them. Other historians consider the Liberals to have benefited. WHY?

Source F

It is true that many grievances co-operated to make the Unionist Party unpopular [but] it is also true that most of these different grievances had some common elements so that they appeared to the electorate like the various counts at a single indictment rather than a number of distinct charges. Thus the attack on Chinese Labour, on Protection, and on the Taff Vale judgement, all formed part of an accusation of plutocratic conspiracy. Even the Education Act was represented as a victory for privilege, and so fell in with the general charge that the Unionists were the party of the rich and selfish who were ready to degrade the British Empire in South Africa by gathering gold through the labour of slaves, to build up a system of monopoly by taxing the food of the poor, to keep the public schools of the nation as a preserve for their own friends and to put the workmen under the heel of the Capitalist by overturning the trade unions. The issues thus seemed to be Rich v. Poor…and it was to no purpose that the Unionist argued one point or another. There was no escaping the general impression – The Unionist Party was branded as the Plutocratic party.

Quarterly Review (April 1906)

Examining the evidence – New Liberalism

The Conservative domination in the late nineteenth century encouraged certain Liberals to adopt a new approach which reflected more progressive attitudes. This New Liberalism was demonstrated at the 1906 Election. It originated with the theories of T.H. Green, an Oxford don who sought to redefine the notion of liberty and the relationship of individual to state. His work, together with that of L.T. Hobhouse, inspired many younger progressive Liberals such as Lloyd George, Hobson, Masterman and Samuel.

Source G

To many among the fathers of modern Liberalism, government action was anathema. They held, as we hold, that the first and final object of the State is to develop the capacities and raise the standard of living of its citizens; but they held also that the best means towards this object was the self-effacement of the state. Liberty is of supreme importance, and legal regulation is the opposite of liberty. Let governments abstain from war, let them practise economy, let them provide proper protection against violence and fraud, let them repeal restrictive laws, and then the free enterprise of commerce will bring prosperity to all classes, while their natural ambitions on the one hand, the pressure of need on the other, will stimulate the hindmost to seek and to attain their own well-being: such was their doctrine. The economics of Adam Smith and the philosophy of Bentham united to found a creed of non-interference which has inspired in large measure the politics of a century. Liberalism became a negative policy, opposing foreign enterprises and entanglements, attacking the laws regulating trade, opinion, combination, land tenure, which had been inherited from a previous generation; its positive proposals were constitutional, aiming at a democratic State structure, and they were constitutional only. If, especially, proposals were made for interfering with the conditions of employment, the Liberals of that generation heard them with suspicion and accepted them, if acceptance was forced by events, with reluctance…

Three causes, then, combined to convert Liberalism from the principle of State abstention. Three causes made possible the adoption of a programme such as that of the recent Liberal government. It was seen that the State had become more efficient and its legislation more competent, and laws of regulation were found by experiment neither to lessen prosperity nor to weaken self-reliance in the manner foretold. It was realised that the conditions of society were in many respects so bad that to tolerate them longer was impossible, and that the *laissez-faire* policy was not likely to bring the cure. And it was realised that extensions of law need not imply diminutions of freedom, but on the contrary would often enlarge freedom.

Such are the facts and arguments which brought about this change. In them we find the answer to those who use the doctrine of the old Liberalism to attack the policy of the new. The State is not incompetent for the work of social reform. Self-reliance is a powerful force, but not powerful enough to cure unaided the diseases that afflict society. Liberty is of supreme importance, but State assistance, rightly directed, may extend the bounds of liberty.

Herbert Samuel, *Liberalism* (1902). Samuel (1870–1963) was elected to parliament as Liberal member for Cleveland in 1902 and served in the Asquith government from 1909 to 1916. Quoted in K.O. Morgan's *The Age of Lloyd George, the Liberal Party and British Politics 1890–1929* (1971)

QUESTIONS ON THE SOURCES

1 According to Herbert Samuel:

(a) what did nineteenth-century Liberals ('the fathers of modern Liberalism') consider to be the role of government?

(b) what reasons are stated for the adoption by government of a more interventionist stance?

(c) what, according to the final sentence, is the essence of New Liberalism?

2 What policies would New Liberals expect a government to carry out?

TASK

Research 'New Liberalism' further, look at its impact on the 1906 election and the new Liberal government which was established. How influential was New Liberalism in the Liberal Party?

Challenging History Resource Pack. Text © Liz Petheram; Illustrations © Thomas Nelson & Sons Ltd; Photographs © as listed on page 2; sourced texts on p. 4. Published by Thomas Nelson & Sons Ltd 1999.

Preview

The General Election of 1900 witnessed the arrival of 15 candidates representing a new parliamentary party – the Labour Party (known as the Labour Representation Committee until 1906). This new political party had only recently been formed in February 1900 at a special conference called by the Trades Union Congress. This conference, held in London, hosted representatives from the wider labour movement including the Fabian Society, the Social Democratic Federation, the Independent Labour Party and the Trade Unions.

The Labour Representation Committee was immediately faced with 'teething' problems over finances, lack of parliamentary representation and experience, a broad spectrum of labour interests, and the decision of many trade unions not to affiliate. Clearly, at such a stage in its career the new party was keen but seriously ill-prepared to fight elections. However, in September 1900 – as the Boer War seemed to be reaching a victorious conclusion for Britain – the Conservative government opportunistically dissolved Parliament and a General Election was called. The Labour Representation Committee polled around 63,000 votes and returned two MPs. Over the next fourteen years the Labour Party grew, but alongside the progress came difficulties and setbacks for the new party.

What were the origins of the Labour Party?

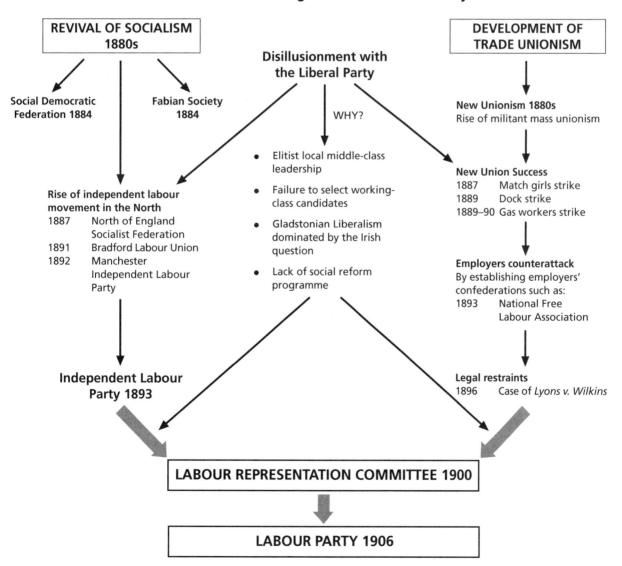

REVIEW OF SOCIALISM 1880s

Social Democratic Federation 1884

Fabian Society 1884

Disillusionment with the Liberal Party

WHY?

- Elitist local middle-class leadership
- Failure to select working-class candidates
- Gladstonian Liberalism dominated by the Irish question
- Lack of social reform programme

DEVELOPMENT OF TRADE UNIONISM

New Unionism 1880s
Rise of militant mass unionism

New Union Success
1887   Match girls strike
1889   Dock strike
1889–90 Gas workers strike

Employers counterattack
By establishing employers' confederations such as:
1893   National Free Labour Association

Rise of independent labour movement in the North
1887   North of England Socialist Federation
1891   Bradford Labour Union
1892   Manchester Independent Labour Party

Independent Labour Party 1893

Legal restraints
1896   Case of *Lyons v. Wilkins*

LABOUR REPRESENTATION COMMITTEE 1900

LABOUR PARTY 1906

Challenging History Resource Pack. Text © Liz Petheram; Illustrations © Thomas Nelson & Sons Ltd; Photographs © as listed on page 2; sourced texts on p. 4. Published by Thomas Nelson & Sons Ltd 1999.

The Early Years 1900–14: setbacks and progress

LABOUR PARTY GROWTH

Election date	Party membership	Seats contested	MPs	% Share of vote
1900	375,931	15	2	1.8
1906	921,280	51	30	5.9
1910 Jan Dec	1,430,539	78 56	40 42	7.6 7.1
(1914)	1,612,147	–	–	–
1918	3,013,129	388	63	22.2

Extracted from Pelling and Reid's *A Short History of the Labour Party* (1961) and Adelman's *The Rise of the Labour Party 1880–1945* (1972)

Talking Point ▼

1 What trends in Labour Party growth do these figures illustrate?

2 Suggest reasons for the changing pace of growth.

Case Study 1

THE TAFF VALE DECISION 1901

Taff Vale Railway v. *Amalgamated Society of Railway Servants*, 1901 (House of Lords Record Office, Opinions of the Law Lords.)

July 22. Lord Macnaughten…

Then, if trade unions are not above the law, the only remaining question, as it seems to me, is one of form. How are these bodies to be sued? I have no doubt whatever that a trade union, whether registered or unregistered, may be sued in a representative action if the persons selected as defendants be persons who, from their position, may be taken fairly to represent the body.

The further question remains: May a registered trade union be sued in and by its registered name? For my part, I cannot see any difficulty in the way of such a suit. It is quite true that a registered trade union is not a corporation, but it has a registered name and a registered office. The registered name is nothing more than a collective name for all the members. The registered office is the place where it carries on business… I can see nothing contrary to principle, or contrary to the provisions of the Trade Union Acts, in holding that a trade union may be sued by its registered name.

I am, therefore, of opinion that the appeal should be allowed and the judgement of Farwell J. restored with costs, here and below.

TASKS

1 How is the impact of each of these case studies reflected in the statistics on Labour Party growth?

2 What difficulties do they illustrate for the new party?

3 Research the Labour Party 1900–14 and complete a full list of problems they encountered.

4 To what extent were these problems overcome?

QUESTIONS

1 What events led to this case being brought before the House of Lords?

2 Explain in your own words the decision taken here by Lord Macnaughten.

3 How did this case affect the growth of the Labour Party?

Challenging History Resource Pack. Text © Liz Petheram; Illustrations © Thomas Nelson & Sons Ltd; Photographs © as listed on page 2; sourced texts on p. 4. Published by Thomas Nelson & Sons Ltd 1999.

Case Study 2

LIB–LAB PACT 1903

Memorandum by Jesse Herbert for
Herbert Gladstone, 6 March 1903
(BL Add. MS. 46025)

…I received an intimation from Mr. George Cadbury that the 'Labour people' were desirous of a friendly arrangement with the Liberal party, by which they might be left free to fight, at the next General Election, in a score or more constituencies, without the rivalry of Liberal candidates. I therefore let Mr. MacDonald, the secretary of the Labour Representation Committee know, by means of a mutual friend, that I would meet him if he wished me to do so. He invited me to meet him on neutral ground and privately, to avoid the comments of those members of his party who are ill disposed towards the Liberal party…

The LRC can directly influence the votes of nearly a million men. They will have a fighting fund of £100,000. (This is the most significant new fact in the situation. Labour candidates have had hitherto to beg for financial help, and have fought with paltry and wholly insufficient funds.) Their members are mainly men who have hitherto voted with the Liberal party. Should they be advised to vote against Liberal candidates, and (as they probably would) should they act as advised, the Liberal party would suffer defeat not only in those constituencies where LRC candidates fought, but also in almost every borough, and in many of the Divisions of Lancashire and Yorkshire. This would be the inevitable result of unfriendly action towards the LRC candidates. They would be defeated, but so also should we be defeated.

Case Study 3

THE OSBORNE JUDGEMENT 1909

Lord Macnaughten

It can hardly be contended that a political organisation is not a thing very different from a combination for trade purposes. There is nothing in any of the Trade Union Acts from which it can be reasonably inferred that trade unions, as defined by Parliament, were ever meant to have the power of collecting and administering funds for political purposes.

Lord Shaw

In brief my opinion is this: The proposed additional rule of the society that 'all candidates shall sign and respect the conditions of the Labour Party, and be subject to their whip', the rule that candidates are to be 'responsible to and paid by the society' and, in particular the provision in the constitution of the Labour Party that 'candidates and members must accept this constitution, and agree to abide by the decision of the parliamentary party in carrying out the aims of the constitution', are all fundamentally illegal, because they are in violation of that sound public policy which is essential to the working of representative government.

Parliament is summoned by the sovereign to advise His Majesty freely. By the nature of the case it is implied that coercion, constraint, or a money payment, which is the price of voting at the bidding of others, destroys or imperils the function of freedom of advice which is fundamental in the very constitution of Parliament. *Inter alia* the Labour Party pledge is such a price, with its accompaniments of unconstitutional and illegal constraint or temptation.

The Law Reports, House of Lords 1910; quoted in Andrew Reekes's *The Rise of Labour 1899–1951* (1991)

QUESTIONS

1 What advantages for the Liberals does Jesse Herbert see in an electoral pact with Labour?

2 Why do you think the Labour Party initiated this discussion?

3 From your research, what was decided in the Lib–Lab electoral pact of 1903?

4 To what extent did it benefit the Labour Party in the 1906 election and afterwards?

QUESTIONS

1 Why was this case known as the Osborne Judgement?

2 What principles as regards the relationship between trade unions and the Labour Party are laid out here by the Law Lords?

3 What was the effect of the Osborne Judgement on the Labour Party in 1910 elections and immediately after?

4 What was the name of the Act which in 1913 reversed the Osborne Judgement? What did it permit trade unions to do in their raising of funds?

Challenging History Resource Pack. Text © Liz Petheram; Illustrations © Thomas Nelson & Sons Ltd; Photographs © as listed on page 2; sourced texts on p. 4. Published by Thomas Nelson & Sons Ltd 1999.

The Who's Who of the Early Labour Party

The first Parliamentary Labour Party, 1906, on the terrace of the House of Commons
Standing, left to right: J. Jenkins, C. W. Bowerman, J. Hodge, J. Parker, G. D. Kelley, W. Hudson, G. J. Wardle, G. N. Barnes, F. W. Jowett, G. H. Roberts, C. Duncan, T. F. Richards, S. Walsh, A. H. Gill, Philip Snowden, T. Summerbell, J. T. Macpherson, T. Glover, J. Seddon, J. R. Clynes, James O'Grady, Will Thorne.
Sitting, left to right: W. T. Wilson, A. Wilkie, J. Ramsay MacDonald, A. Henderson, J. Keir Hardie, D. J. Shackleton, Will Crooks

JAMES KEIR HARDIE (1856–1915)

Keir Hardie, often labelled the 'Father of the Labour Party', was born into poverty in Lanarkshire, Scotland. He was self-educated, becoming a trade union organiser, journalist, propagandist, MP and internationally famous socialist. He was elected Independent Socialist MP for West Ham South in 1892, arriving at Westminster in deerstalker and tweed jacket.

Hardie founded the ILP in 1893, played a leading role in the formation of the LRC in 1900, and became chairman and leader of the parliamentary party in 1906. He sat as MP for Merthyr Tydfil from 1900 to 1915. Hardie possessed charisma yet remained true to his roots, espousing the cause of the poor and deprived. He was a fervent non-conformist and pacifist.

Keir Hardie

J. RAMSAY MacDONALD (1866–1937)

Ramsay MacDonald

Ramsay MacDonald was also born into poverty in Scotland and similarly was self-educated, working his way to the top. On joining the ILP in 1894 he was found to be a good organiser, contributing significantly to the Lib–Lab Pact agreed in 1903. He became an MP in 1906 and was chairman of the ILP. In 1911 he took over from Keir Hardie as leader of the parliamentary party until 1914, when his pacifism caused him to resign in favour of Henderson.

Although defeated in the 1918 elections, he was returned in 1922 as MP for Aberavon and promptly re-elected as leader of the parliamentary party. He remained Leader of the Opposition until Labour formed its first minority ministry in 1924. MacDonald became Prime Minister in January and, although defeated in November 1924, he became PM again in 1929, forming a coalition – the National Government – in 1931. He resigned in 1935 and was succeeded by the Conservative leader, Stanley Baldwin.

Challenging History Resource Pack. Text © Liz Petheram; Illustrations © Thomas Nelson & Sons Ltd; Photographs © as listed on page 2; sourced texts on p. 4. Published by Thomas Nelson & Sons Ltd 1999.

POVERTY AND SOCIAL REFORM 1900–14

Preview

The Liberal government after 1906 tackled the issue of poverty in Britain by passing a large package of social reform. This legislation set a precedent in social welfare by making the government responsible for providing help to some of the most vulnerable sections of society – children, the aged, the unemployed or sick worker. Was this social reform motivated by the Liberal government's humanitarian concern for the poor or were there equally important political pressures?

A slum household – living in one room c.1910

Source A

'The Poverty Trap'

The life of a labourer is marked by five alternating periods of want and comparative plenty. During early childhood, unless his father is a skilled worker, he probably will be in poverty; this will last until he, or some of his brothers or sisters begin to earn money and thus augment their father's wage sufficiently to raise the family above the poverty line. Then follows the period during which he is earning money and living under his parents' roof; for some portion of this period he will be earning more money than is required for lodging, food, and clothes. This is his chance to save money. If he has saved enough to pay for furnishing a cottage, this period of comparative prosperity may continue after marriage until he has two or three children, when poverty will again overtake him. This period of poverty will last perhaps for ten years, i.e. until the first child is fourteen years old and begins to earn wages; but if there are more than three children it may last longer. While the children are earning, and before they leave the home to marry, the man enjoys another period of prosperity – possibly, however, only to sink back again into poverty when his children have married and left him, and he himself is too old to work, for his income has never permitted his saving enough for him and his wife to live upon for more than a very short time…

B.S. Rowntree, *Poverty, a Study in Town Life* (1902); quoted in K. Benning's *Edwardian Britain* (1980)

Source B

These are descriptions of families visited by Rowntree's investigators. They are from those whose total income was less than 22 shillings (110p) a week.

i) No occupation. Married. Age sixty-four. Two rooms. The man 'has not had his boots on' for twelve months. He is suffering from dropsy. His wife cleans schools. This house shares one closet [W.C.] with eight other houses, and one water tap with four others. Rent 2s 6d [12½p].

ii) Joiner. Married. Four Rooms. Six children. Poor and untidy. Infant very sickly. Buried two children within two years. Husband often on short time; reason given, 'Company's arrangements'. Mother often ill, though looking healthy and cheerful. Rent 3s 8½d [18p].

iii) Odd jobs. Age sixty-five. One room. Formerly grocer's assistant, dismissed on account of age. Very poor, intelligent, and respectable; room clean and tidy. This house shares one closet and one water tap with three other houses. Rent 2s 6d [12½p].

B.S. Rowntree, *Poverty, a Study in Town Life* (1902)

Talking Point ▼

1 How is poverty dealt with in contemporary society?

2 What were the main causes of poverty in Edwardian Britain?

Liberal Social Reforms 1906–11 motivated by

REASONS FOR LIBERAL SOCIAL REFORM

Poverty exposed demand for reform

Source C

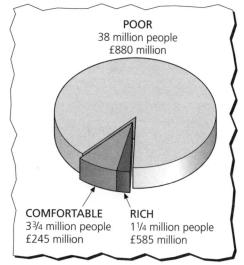

POOR
38 million people
£880 million

COMFORTABLE
3¾ million people
£245 million

RICH
1¼ million people
£585 million

1904 Distribution of income in UK of approximately £1,710,000 among population of 43 million, according to L.G. Chiozza *Money, Riches and Poverty* (1905)

Source D

Darkest England may be described as consisting broadly of three circles, one within the other. The outer and widest circle is inhabited by the starving and homeless, but honest, Poor. The second by those who live by Vice; and the third and innermost region at the centre is peopled by those who exist by Crime. The whole of the three circles is sodden with Drink…

The borders of this great lost land are not sharply defined. They are continually expanding or contracting. Whenever there is a period of depression in trade, they stretch; when prosperity returns, they contract. So far as individuals are concerned, there are none among the hundreds of thousands who live upon the outskirts of the dark forest who can truly say that they or their children are secure from being hopelessly entangled in its labyrinth. The death of the breadwinner, a long illness, a failure in the city, or any one of a thousand other causes which might be named, will bring within the first circle those who at present imagine themselves free from all danger of actual want.

William Booth, *In Darkest England and the Way Out* (1890)

Lloyd George – radical reformer

Source E

I never said this bill was a final solution. I am not putting it forward as a complete remedy. It is one of a series. We are advancing on the road, but it is an essential part of the journey. I have been now some years in politics and I have had, I think, as large a share of contention and strife and warfare as any man in British politics today. This year, this Session, I have joined the Red Cross. I am in the ambulance corps. I am engaged to drive a wagon through the twistings and turnings and ruts of the Parliamentary road. There are men who tell me I have overloaded that wagon. I have taken three years to pack it carefully. I cannot spare a single parcel, for the suffering is very great. There are those who say my wagon is half empty. I say it is as much as I can carry. Now there are some who say I am in a great hurry. I am rather in a hurry, for I can hear the moanings of the wounded, and I want to carry relief to them in the alleys, the homes where they lie stricken, and I ask you, and through you, I ask the millions of good-hearted men and women who constitute the majority of the people of this land – I ask you to help me to set aside hindrances, to overcome obstacles, to avoid the pitfalls that beset my difficult path.

Extract from Lloyd George's 'Ambulance Wagon' speech at Birmingham from *The Times*, 12 June 1911; quoted in Fraser's *Evolution of the Welfare State* (1973) © Times Newspapers Limited, London 1911, [Photocopying allowed for classroom use only]

Source F

Punch cartoon, 1908

PUNCH, OR THE LONDON CHARIVARI, August 5, 1908.

OLD AGE PENSION FUND

THE PHILANTHROPIC HIGHWAYMAN.
MR. LLOYD-GEORGE. *"I'LL* MAKE 'EM PITY THE AGED POOR!"

Development of new liberalism

Source G

It was realised that the conditions of society were in many respects so bad that to tolerate them longer was impossible, and that the *laissez-faire* policy was not likely to bring the cure. And it was realised that extensions of law need not imply diminutions of freedom, but on the contrary would often enlarge freedom.

Such are the facts and arguments which brought about this change. In them we find the answer to those who use the doctrine of the old Liberalism to attack the policy of the new. The State is not incompetent for the work of social reform. Self-reliance is a powerful force, but not powerful enough to cure unaided the diseases that afflict society. Liberty is of supreme importance, but State assistance, rightly directed, may extend the bounds of liberty…

Herbert Samuel *Liberalism* (1902)

Source H

It is certain that as we enter upon these untrodden fields of British politics we shall need the aid of every moral and religious force which is alive in England to-day. Sacrifices will be required from every class in the population; the rich must contribute in money and the poor in service, if their children are to tread a gentler path towards a fairer goal. A fiscal system which prudently but increasingly imposes the necessary burdens of the State upon unearned wealth will not only be found capable of providing the funds which will be needed, but will also stimulate enterprise and production. And thus from many quarters we may work towards the establishment of that Minimum Standard below which competition cannot be allowed, but above which it may continue healthy and free, to vivify and fertilise the world.

It is because the influence of *The Nation* may be powerful to aid further these causes, that I send you my good wishes and congratulations to-day. – I am, Sir,

Yours faithfully,
Winston S. Churchill.

W.S. Churchill, 'The Untrodden Field of Politics' from *The Nation* (7 March 1908)

Sources G and H quoted from K. O. Morgan's *The Age of Lloyd George, the Liberal Party and British Politics 1890–1929* (1971)

Challenging History Resource Pack. Text © Liz Petheram; Illustrations © Thomas Nelson & Sons Ltd; Photographs © as listed on page 2; sourced texts on p. 4. Published by Thomas Nelson & Sons Ltd 1999.

humanitarian concern or political pragmatism?

Threat to the Liberals by the Labour Party

Source I

> Socialism wants to pull down wealth, Liberalism seeks to raise up poverty... Socialism assails the maximum pre-eminence of the individual – Liberalism seeks to build up the minimum standard of the masses.

Extract from speech, Winston Churchill 1908; quoted in Hopkin's *Social History of the English Working Classes* (1979)

Source J

> But I have one word for Liberals. I can tell them what will make this I.L.P. movement a great and sweeping force in this country – a course that will sweep away Liberalism amongst other things. If at the end of an average term of office it were found that a Liberal Parliament had done nothing to cope seriously with the social condition of the people, to remove the national degradation of slums and widespread poverty and destitution in a land glittering with wealth; that they had shrunk from attacking boldly the causes of this wretchedness, notably the drink and this vicious land system; that they had not arrested the waste of our national resources in armaments, nor provided an honourable sustenance for deserving old age; that they had tamely allowed the House of Lords to extract all the virtue out of their Bills so that the Liberal statute book remained simply a bundle of sapless legislative faggots fit only for the fire; then would a real cry arise in this land for a new party, and many of us here in this room would join in that cry. But if a Liberal Government tackle the landlords, and the brewers, and the peers, as they have faced the parsons, and try to deliver the nation from the pernicious control of this confederacy of monopolists, then the Independent Labour Party will call in vain upon the working men of Britain to desert Liberalism that is so gallantly fighting to rid the land of the wrongs that have oppressed those who labour in it.

Lloyd George in a speech at Cardiff, 11 October 1906; quoted in K. Benning's *Edwardian Britain* (1980)

Source K

PUNCH, OR THE LONDON CHARIVARI—October 27, 1909.

FORCED FELLOWSHIP.

SUSPICIOUS-LOOKING PARTY. "ANY OBJECTION TO MY COMPANY, GUV'NOR? I'M AGOIN' YOUR WAY"—*(aside)* "AND FURTHER."

Punch cartoon, 1909

TASKS

1 What evidence do these sources offer to support the various reasons for Liberal Social Reform?

2 Research further each of these factors and explain why they promoted social legislation.

3 Identify which you consider to be the most important factor and argue the case with evidence in a class discussion.

Concern for national efficiency

Source L

> What is the use of talking about Empire if here, at its very centre, there is always to be found a mass of people, stunted in education, a prey of intemperance, huddled and congested beyond the possibility of realising in any true sense either social or domestic life?

Asquith 1905; quoted in Hopkin's *Social History of the English Working Classes* (1979)

Source M

> **The German Example**
> When introducing the budget Lloyd George had spoken with enthusiasm of the German system of social insurance. Feeling between the two countries was rising and the heavy naval estimates which the budget had to cover were dictated by the concern for Britain's security at sea which had produced the costly *Dreadnought*. There were, nevertheless, other aspects of policy in which, Lloyd George insisted, "we must put ourselves on a level with Germany":
> I hope our competition with Germany will not be in armaments alone.
> The great insurance scheme of 1911, which the 1909 budget made possible, was, apart from the unique British institution of unemployment insurance, directly inspired by the German model. As has already been mentioned, Lloyd George was not aware of the insurance proposals of the Majority Report of the Poor Law Commission until his own plans were well advanced. In the summer of 1908, however, he had spent some time in Germany seeing for himself the working of the German insurance system, and his mind had in any case been turned towards insurance as a result of his experience in steering old age pensions through the Commons. The amendments that had been proposed to him would have cost, he estimated, more than sixty million pounds: whatever else was to be added to pensions could not therefore be conceived of as an outright charge on the State. He returned from Germany, as he acknowledged, "tremendously impressed" by what he had seen, especially by the great improvements that had been effected in the conditions of the people at small cost to the State. Here was a model for what he wished to do in Britain, and he sent officials to study it in more detail.

Maurice Bruce, *The Coming of the Welfare State* (1961)

Liberal Social Legislation 1906–11

Date	Legislation	Implementation	Limitations and other consideratons
1906	Education (Provision of Meals) Act	Local authorities were empowered to raise ½d rate to finance meals for needy schoolchildren.	• Introduced by a Labour MP although supported by government. • Authorities not compelled to provide meals – limited number in fact did. • Government grant not until 1914 – only covered half the cost. • Imperialist motive after poor standard of Boer War recruits.
1907	Education (Administrative Provisions) Act	A medical department set up within the Board of Education which was to ensure the provision of a school medical service. School clinics were introduced.	• Result of back-bench pressure in face of significant Liberal opposition. • As above, motivated by Imperial concern for military effectiveness and national efficiency.
1908	Children Act	Established formally the legal rights of a child. Parental negligence was made illegal. Borstals, remand houses and juvenile courts were set up to deal with young offenders.	• Largely a codifying Act covering a wide area of concerns. • Has been termed the 'Children's Charter'.
1908	Old Age Pensions Act	A non-contributory scheme for payment of 5s [25p] per week at the age of 70. Pensions were to be paid through the Post Office.	• Pensions were kept small and were not intended to replace savings. • Until 1911 pensions paid only to those considered 'deserving poor'. • Pensions paid only to those with incomes less than £31 p.a. • Estimated cost in 1908 was £6m. Cost by 1913 was £12m.
1909	Trade Boards Act	Minimum wages established in the sweated trades.	• Criticised as curtailing freedom of master and worker.
1911	National Insurance Act Part 1 – Health	Compulsory insurance against sickness for all earning up to £160 p.a. Employee to pay 4d, employer 3d and state 2d. Entitlement – 10s [50p] sickness benefit and free medical care. Maternity benefit – 30s [£1.50] and help to enter TB sanatorium.	• Concern for national efficiency. • Model for this scheme taken from Germany. • Lack of hospital provision. • Failed to include dependants for medical treatment. • Criticised by trade unions for making deductions from already low wages.
	Part 2 – Unemployment	Compulsory insurance against unemployment. Employer and employee to pay 2½d per week plus 1⅔d from state. Entitlement 7s [35p] per week for 15 weeks.	• Benefits were small and for limited period. • Only for certain trades of building, engineers, iron workers. • Men dismissed for misconduct deprived of benefit. • No further expansion of scheme until 1920.

TASKS

1 To what extent did these reforms help the groups in society who were most vulnerable to poverty?

2 What do you understand by the phrase 'The Welfare State'?

3 How far do you consider the Liberal government's social reforms 1906–11 contributed towards establishing a welfare state in Britain?

Challenging History Resource Pack. Text © Liz Petheram; Illustrations © Thomas Nelson & Sons Ltd; Photographs © as listed on page 2; sourced texts on p. 4. Published by Thomas Nelson & Sons Ltd 1999.

THE 1909 PEOPLE'S BUDGET AND CONSTITUTIONAL CRISIS

Preview

In 1909 Lloyd George, the Liberal Chancellor, introduced a budget to raise increased revenue for social reform and defence. Its controversial nature sparked a constitutional crisis over the power of the House of Lords. After two years of wrangling which involved the two Houses of Parliament, the media, two kings and two General Elections, the matter was resolved by the passing of the Parliament Act in 1911.

Main proposals of the 1909 Budget

Proposal

1. Increase in income tax by 2d to 1s 2d in £ on unearned income over £700 and earned incomes above £2,000.

2. Supertax of 6d in £ on incomes over £5,000 payable on the income above £3,000.

3. 20% tax on the unearned increased value of land when it changes ownership.

4. 1d in £ tax on capital value of all land worth over £50 an acre.

5. 3d levy on a gallon of petrol and introduction of licences for motor-cars.

6. Higher taxes on tobacco and spirits (a bottle of whisky rose from 3s 6d to 4s).

7. Rise in cost of liquor licences paid by publicans and brewers.

8. Additional death duties.

TASKS

1 How did this Budget, introduced by Chancellor Lloyd George, mark a break with traditional Budgetary policy?

2 What reasons did Lloyd George have for introducing such a Budget?

3 Why was it rejected by the House of Lords?

4 Explain why the rejection of this Budget led to a constitutional crisis.

Talking Point ▼

Did Lloyd George deliberately provoke, by means of a controversial Budget, a confrontation with the House of Lords which would lead to its reform?

Source A

"In their indignation against Lloyd George's methods – the Lords fell into the trap which he deliberately prepared for them."

L.S. Amery, *My Political Life* (1953)

Source B

"This is a War Budget. It is for raising money to wage implacable War against poverty and squalidness."

Lloyd George, speech in the House of Commons, 29 April 1909, *Hansard*

Source C

"I have seen it stated that the Budget was a strategic ruse deliberately framed to provoke the House of Lords into rejecting it, thus digging their own graves... I can vouch for the fact that as far as my father [H. Asquith] was concerned there is not a vestige of truth in this suggestion."

Lady Violet Bonham-Carter, *Winston Churchill as I Knew Him* (1965) quoted in Benning (1980)

Source D

"I'm not so sure we ought to pray for it to go through. I'm not so sure we ought not to hope for its rejection. It would give us such a chance as we shall never have again."

Lloyd George in conversation with Masterman, HiDES

Challenging History Resource Pack. Text © Liz Petheram; Illustrations © Thomas Nelson & Sons Ltd; Photographs © as listed on page 2; sourced texts on p. 4. Published by Thomas Nelson & Sons Ltd 1999.

Examining the evidence

Source E

In all seriousness, my Lords, we have a right to ask where this kind of thing is going to stop. If you can graft Licensing Bills and Land Valuation Bills and measures of that kind on the Finance Bill, what is to prevent you grafting on it, let us say, a Home Rule Bill – setting up an authority in Ireland to collect and dispense all the taxes of that country? There is literally no limit to the abuses which might creep in if such a practice were allowed to go on without restriction. Upon this ground alone I venture to think your Lordship's House might consider very seriously whether you are justified in passing this Bill into Law…

I trust…I have said enough to show your Lordships that the question before you is not whether you *can* reject this Bill but whether you *ought* to reject this Bill – a wholly different thing. You have to consider its results as they would affect all classes of the community, and the principles that underlie it, and you have to consider whether the people of this country have been consulted with regard to it. If you find that the results are likely to be disastrous and that the principles underlying it, which we detect not only from the official utterance of members of the Government but also from the more indiscreet explanations of so-called supporters of the Government are pernicious and that the whole matter is one that has never been duly referred to the people of this country, then I venture to say that your Lordships have a clear duty before you – not to decree the final extinction of the Bill – because that is not what we propose, but to insist that before it becomes law an authoritative expression of the opinion of the electors of the United Kingdom shall have reached us with regard to it…

We shall be asked whether we have considered the consequences of rejecting the Budget. My Lords, we have considered them, and we are ready to face them…

We are told to think well of the consequences to this House. That is conveyed to us in various tones, sometimes full of solicitude, and sometimes minatory and violent. It is in effect intimated to us that as the penalty of rejecting this Bill we are to expect an attempt to deprive this House of its constitutional rights of dealing with Money Bills . . . I am not greatly alarmed by these threats. I recall to mind that, before the Budget was dreamt of, the same threats were held over our heads. We were told long before this Budget could even have been thought of by its authors that the question of curtailment of the rights of the House of Lords was to be the dominant issue at the next election . . . We are therefore justified in assuming that, whatever happens, this struggle has got to come. What I would venture to ask those noble Lords . . . is this – Shall we stand better or shall we stand worse when the struggle comes if we shirk our responsibility now?

Lord Lansdowne, in a speech on the 1909 Budget to the House of Lords in November 1909. *Hansard Parliamentary Debates*, 5th series, vol. iv, col. 731–50

Source F

The object of a second chamber is not, and never has been, to prevent the people, the mass of the community, the electorate, the constituencies determining what policy they should pursue; it exists for the purpose of seeing that on great issues the policy which is pursued is not the policy of a temporary majority elected for a different purpose, but represents the sovereign conviction of the people for the few years in which it carries their mandate…its mission and great function is to see that the Government of this country is a popular Government. What it has to do on these fortunately rare, but all the more important, occasions is not to insist that this or that minority, powerful for the time, once powerful perhaps, no longer powerful it may be, is to be clothed with all the tyrannical powers which we have done so much to prevent anybody in the State, any element in the State, exercising. The object is to see that there shall be referred to the people that which concerns the people; and that the people shall not be betrayed by hasty legislation, interested legislation, legislation having, it may be, some electoral object in view, or some vindictive policy to carry out.

A.J. Balfour in a speech at Manchester reported in *The Times* 18 November 1909 quoted in Benning (1980); © Times Newspaper Limited, London 1909, [Photocopying allowed for classroom use only]

Punch cartoon, 1908

STANDING FOR HIS TRADE PHOTOGRAPH (CHRISTMAS AND NEW YEAR SEASON, 1908-9). (Lord L-nsd-wne.)

TASKS

1 Read the sources carefully and identify the arguments put forward in the debate over the power of the House of Lords.

2 Divide the sources into the two camps: Peers/Conservatives and People/Liberals.

3 Research the debate further and write a speech for each side incorporating the main arguments.

Peers v. People Debate

Source G

Today will be signalised by an event of the highest constitutional and historical importance – the exercise by the House of Lords of an unquestionable and indispensable right which it has not been necessary to use for a very long time, thanks to the wise moderation with which, upon the whole, our Constitution has been worked by statement of all parties. That traditional moderation, without which an unwritten Constitution is an impossible contrivance has been abandoned by the present Government; and the House of Lords has accordingly been compelled either to fall back upon the use of a weapon reserved for dire emergencies or to submit to effacement as an efficient Second Chamber…

There is no precedent for a Government avowedly pursuing the policy of destroying the power of the House of Lords to reject or amend any measure that a temporary majority in the Commons may be pleased to pass, whether that measure be desired or disliked by the country. But that and nothing else, has been the declared policy of the present Government, and the Budget is merely the culmination of a design deliberately adopted and steadily pursued.

The Times, 30 November 1909; quoted in Benning (1980); © Times Newspapers Limited, London 1909, [Photocopying allowed for classroom use only]

Source H

A fully-equipped duke costs as much to keep up as two 'Dreadnoughts', and they are just as great a terror, and they last longer. As long as they were contented to be mere idols on their pedestals, preserving that stately silence which became their rank and their intelligence, all went well, and the average British citizen rather looked up to them, and said to himself, 'Well, if the worst comes to the worst for this old country, we have always got the dukes to fall back on.'

But then came the Budget, the dukes stepped off their perch. They have been scolding like omnibus drivers purely because the Budget cart has knocked a little of the gilt off their old stage coach. Well, we cannot put them back again…

Let them realise what they are doing. They are forcing a revolution, and they will get it. The Lords may decree a revolution, but the people will direct it. If they begin, issues will be raised that they little dream of. Questions will be asked which are now whispered in humble voices, and answers will be demanded then with authority. The question will be asked whether five hundred men, ordinary men chosen accidentally from among the unemployed, should override the judgement – the deliberate judgement – of millions of people who are engaged in the industry which makes the wealth of the country.

D. Lloyd George in a speech at Newcastle, reported in *The Times* 11 October 1909; quoted in Benning (1980); © Times Newspapers Limited, London 1909, [Photocopying allowed for classroom use only]

Daily Dispatch, April 1, 1910

FIRST WHOLLY UNSUSPICIOUS CHARACTER: "If we so much as lay our 'ands on the gate 'e rouses the whole 'ousehold. It's downright tyranny—that's wot it is!"

Source I

The truth is that all this talk about the duty or the right of the House of Lords to refer measures to the people is, in the light of our practical and actual experience, the hollowest outcry of political cant… It is simply a thin rhetorical veneer, by which it is sought to gloss over the partisan, and in this case the unconstitutional, action of the purely partisan Chamber. The sum and substance of the matter is that the House of Lords rejected the Finance Bill last Tuesday, not because they love the people, but because they hate the Budget…

The real question which emerges from the political struggles in this country for the last 30 years is not whether you will have a single or a double chamber system of government, but whether when the Tory Party is in power the House of Commons shall be omnipotent, and whether when the Liberal Party is in power the House of Lords shall be omnipotent.

We are living under a system of false balances and loaded dice. When the democracy votes Tory we are submitted to the uncontrolled domination of a single Chamber. When the democracy votes Liberal, a dormant Second Chamber wakes up from its slumbers and is able to frustrate and nullify our efforts, as it did with regard to education, as it did with regard to licensing, as it has done again this year with regard to measures from Scotland, and with regard to finance. I cannot exhaust the list; it would be too long. They proceed to frustrate and nullify the clearest and most plainly expressed intention of the elective House. The House of Lords have deliberately chosen their ground. They have elected to set at nought in regard to finance the unwritten and time-honoured conventions of our Constitution. In so doing, whether they foresaw it or not, they have opened out a wider and a more far reaching issue. We have not provoked the challenge, but we welcome it.

H.H. Asquith, in a speech to the House of Commons, 2 December 1909 *Hansard Parliamentary Debates*, 5th series, vol. 13, col. 557–8

Reform of the House of Lords, 1911

RECORD OF EVENTS

1909

April 29	– Lloyd George introduces Budget in House of Commons.
May–November	– Commons debate Budget. 554 divisions.
	– Budget Protest League and Budget League formed.
November	– Budget passes Commons (379–149 votes).
	– Lords reject Budget (350–75 votes).

1910

January	– General Election (Liberals 275, Conservatives 273, Labour 40, Irish 82).
April	– Parliament Bill to reform Lords passes Commons.
	– Budget approved by Lords.
May	– Death of Edward VII; accession of George V.
June	
July	– Conference meets to reach solution.
August	
November	– Lords reject Parliament Bill.
	– King promises new peers.
December	– General Election (Liberals 272, Conservatives 272, Irish 84, Labour 42).

1911

May	– Parliament Bill passes Commons.
July	– Asquith's announcement of King's intention to create 500 Liberal peers.
	– Lords split into 'Hedgers and Ditchers' over the problem.
August	– Parliament Bill passes Lords (131–114).

Talking Point ▼

Was reform needed?

The House of Lords, although not elected, had the power to veto any legislation which had passed the Commons. Traditionally, however, they had never rejected the Budget. During the latter part of the nineteenth century the House of Lords, with its Conservative majority, continually rejected Liberal bills although it did not interfere with Conservative legislation.

1893	Gladstone's second Irish Home Rule Bill	**REJECTED!**
1906	Liberal Education Bill	**REJECTED!**
	Plural Voting Bill	**REJECTED!**
1908	Licensing Bill	**REJECTED!**
	Old Age Pension	**PLANNED TO REJECT!**

Parliament Act 1911

❶ The Lords were not allowed to reject or amend a finance bill. The speaker of the House of Commons was to decide which were finance bills.

❷ The Lords could amend and reject other bills until they had passed the Commons three times in which case they automatically became law.

❸ General Elections should be held every five instead of every seven years.

Members of Parliament were awarded salaries in the same year.

Is reform needed now?

TASKS

1   What is the composition of the House of Lords now?

2   Is a second House a necessary part of a democratic system?

3   Would you either reform or abolish the House of Lords, or maintain the status quo?

Challenging History Resource Pack. Text © Liz Petheram; Illustrations © Thomas Nelson & Sons Ltd; Photographs © as listed on page 2; sourced texts on p. 4. Published by Thomas Nelson & Sons Ltd 1999.

Preview

Unrest amongst the industrial workforce in Britain presented the Liberal government with significant problems in the period 1910–13. The strike wave involved stoppages by miners, dockers, railway workers, cotton workers and boilermakers. Increased industrial action is illustrated by the figures:

- Number of stoppages/strikes
  1906 – 478   1913 – 1,459

- Working days lost
  1907 – 2,150,000   1913 – 40,890,000

How healthy was the British economy at this time?

POSITIVE SIGNS

1. Total industrial production was growing and reached a peak in 1913.
2. Balance of payments enjoyed a healthy surplus of £239 million.
3. Britain's international position was still central in trading affairs.
4. There was diversification into tertiary industries such as shipping, insurance and world banking.
5. There was an increased supply of South African gold.
6. The economy was stimulated by demands for materials to supply the arms race.

PROBLEMS FACING BRITISH INDUSTRY

Textiles

- Britain remained the predominant textile producer in Europe. However, competition was developing in the USA and the Far East.
- There was technical stagnation – for example in the spinning process, over 80% of cotton was spun with mule spindles, not the newer ring spindle.
- Due to more intense competition from abroad, Britain resorted to selling an increasing number of goods to 'soft' markets such as India.
- Numbers employed in the textile trade were declining faster than in any other occupation.

Iron and steel

- Output in Britain was overtaken by the USA and Germany – in 1913 output stood at: Britain 5 million tons, the USA 13 million tons, Germany 13 million tons.
- British industry was not protected by trade barriers as were other countries.
- Dissatisfaction amongst the workforce was caused by an erosion of craft privileges and the spread of piecework.
- Railways' running costs increased, yet charges for goods were kept low.

Agriculture

- Investment decreased – between 1880 and 1914, net investment in livestock buildings was negative.
- Output stagnated and the contribution of agriculture to the national income fell.
- By 1895, 77% of wheat consumed was imported, and this figure rose up to 1914.
- The agricultural population continued to decline.

Mining

- Export figures were lower than in the USA and Germany. In 1913, output stood at: Britain 287 million tons per annum, the USA 500 million tons per annum.
- Old coal seams were being worked out – in 1913 two-thirds of all coal came from collieries established before 1875.
- Through lack of investment and innovation, the coal industry failed to introduce steel pit props, electrical haulage and mechanical coal cutters, and to open new seams.
- From 1890 onwards the other mining industries such as lead, tin and zinc were virtually wiped out.

Challenging History Resource Pack. Text © Liz Petheram; Illustrations © Thomas Nelson & Sons Ltd; Photographs © as listed on page 2; sourced texts on p. 4. Published by Thomas Nelson & Sons Ltd 1999.

The Strike Wave 1910–13
A nation of contrasts

Source A

Underneath our gay social life... the Boat Race, the Epsom races, Henley, Ascot, Cowes, cricket at Lords, the massed mobs at professional football matches, tennis tournaments, music and mirth at the White City – there were signs and sudden outbreaks of ugly conflict. Labour for millions of men and women... was underpaid, overworked and insecure.

Sir Philip Gibbs, *The Pageant of the Years* (1946); quoted in Benning (1980)

1910

February–November

Miners' strike – 30,000 men involved; rioting breaks out.

Churchill delays army intervention. No deaths. (Tonypandy)

July

Railway strike. (Tyneside)

September

Cotton trades, stoppage settled by the Board of Trade. (Accrington)

September–December

Boilermakers' strike. (Tyneside)

1911

June

Ten-day strike of seamen and firemen.

Shipping magnates give way and concede all demands. (Southampton)

August

Dock strike – 20,000 men out for eleven days – settled. (London)

National rail strike

Rioting; two men shot dead by troops whilst looting shops and a train. (Llanelli, S. Wales)

Dock strike – riot quelled by troops. Two men killed. (Liverpool)

December

Strike of 126,000 weavers, settled by a truce.

£1 million lost in wages. (Accrington)

15,000 Bermondsey women sweatshop workers on strike. (London)

1912

March–April

Miners' confederation calls a strike for minimum wage.

Two million men called out.

May

Dock strike – government refuse to intervene.

Strike collapses after a month. (London)

1913

Strike by transport workers in Dublin.

Small-scale disputes in Midlands metal trades.

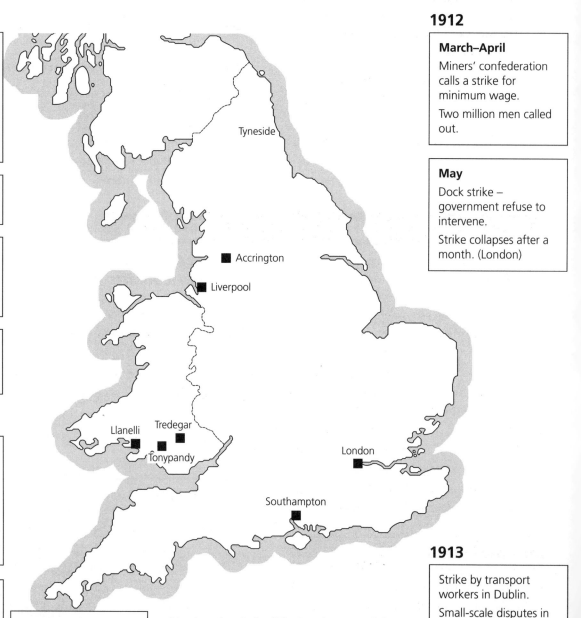

Map based on Pollard The Development of the British Economy 1914–15 *(1963)*

TASK

Using the material on pages 21 and 22 and other reading you have done, write a brief summary of the nature of industrial unrest in this period. Consider: union organisation, the actions of strikers and government, numbers involved and geographical location.

Challenging History Resource Pack. Text © Liz Petheram; Photographs © as listed on page 2; sourced texts on p. 4. Published by Thomas Nelson & Sons Ltd 1999.

TASK

Essay Why was there labour unrest in Britain 1910–13?

Plan and write the above essay. First, find out more information about each of the suggested causes and fill in the 'Evidence' section. Consider the importance of each cause below to labour unrest.

Causes	Evidence
• Decline in traditional industries and the emergence of complaints specific to individual trades.	
• Development of New Unionism in the late 1880s.	
• Working conditions and the introduction of new machinery caused adjustment, job losses and employee–employer conflict.	
• 1909–13 Prices rose more rapidly than wages. Cost of living increased.	
• Trade union dissatisfaction with the government and law courts over the legal rights of unions.	
• Retaliatory action against union activity by the employers since late nineteenth century.	
• Emergence of Syndicalism.	
• Liberal government's 1906 Trade Disputes Act disappointed the unions by its limitations, yet enabled them to take strike action without the fear of prosecution.	
• Unemployment fell after 1910, increasing bargaining power in the competitive labour market.	
• A transferable momentum of strikes built up from one industry to another.	

Challenging History Resource Pack. Text © Liz Petheram; Illustrations © Thomas Nelson & Sons Ltd; Photographs © as listed on page 2; sourced texts on p. 4. Published by Thomas Nelson & Sons Ltd 1999.

What were the consequences of the industrial unrest?

GOVERNMENT

- Developed a policy which aimed to firmly maintain law and order in addition to dealing with disputes as arbitrator.

- Board of Trade appointed mediators to intervene when requested in a dispute. G.R. Askwith, Chief Industrial Commissioner from 1911, negotiated settlements in numerous disputes with dockers and cotton workers.

- Permanent conciliation boards were established, numbers increasing from 162 in 1905 to 325 in 1913.

- Industrial Council was set up in 1911 as a national body to bring together employers and trade union representatives.

- Personal intervention of Lloyd George and Winston Churchill was skilful, conciliatory and restraining.

WORKFORCE

- Amongst the workers, there developed an increased awareness of the power of unionised labour.

- Membership of trade unions rose:
  1909 – 2½ million
  1911 – 3 million   } approximately
  1912 – 3½ million
  1913 – 4 million

- Centralised organisation developed amongst unionists:
  1910 – National Transport Workers' Federation was formed.
  1913 – National Union of Railwaymen was formed.

- The philosophy of Syndicalism spread. Its aim was to gain control of industry for workers, through the co-operation of different industries in a 'general strike'. Tom Mann was the main exponent, helping to produce the newspaper *Syndicalist* in 1912 and the influential 'The Miners' Next Step'.

- Benefited from the government's social and trade union reform.

LEGISLATION

- An interventionist policy was pursued both before and after the labour unrest.

  Before:
  1906 – Trade Disputes Act
  1908 – Mines 8 Hours Act
  1909 – Trade Boards Act

  After:
  1911 – Salary for MPs
  1912 – Miners' Minimum Wage Act – a compromise piece of legislation between miners' demands and pressure from coal owners
  1913 – Trade Union Act – reversed the Osborne Judgement. Allowed trade unions to raise a political fund but separately from that for industrial purposes. Workers were able to contract out of paying the political levy.

Talking Point ▼

1 Did industrial unrest in this period demonstrate a changing relationship between 'labour' and government? Consider the causes, nature and consequences of this unrest.

2 Do you think the Liberal government was damaged by the conflict?

THE WOMEN'S SUFFRAGE MOVEMENT: LATE NINETEENTH CENTURY TO 1914

Preview

By 1900 a women's suffrage movement had developed centred around the National Union of Women's Suffrage Societies led by Millicent Fawcett. This was contributed to by social, economic and political development for women in late nineteenth-century society.

In 1903 a more assertive and increasingly militant splinter group was formed – the Women's Social and Political Union led by Emmeline Pankhurst, commonly known as the Suffragettes.

This group gained much publicity at the time, but did their campaign **hinder** or **help** their cause?

Timeline

1979	First female Prime Minister in Britain – Margaret Thatcher.
1975	Sex Discrimination Act made gender discrimination illegal in areas such as employment.
1971	Equal Pay Act attempted pay comparability with men.
1969	Votes for females and males over 18.
1929	First female Cabinet member – Margaret Bondfield, Labour MP.
1928	Votes for females over 21.
1919	First female MP to sit in the House – Nancy, Lady Astor.
1918	Votes for females over 30.

Changes in working life for women

- Increase in the number of women entering the professions, for example in 1900 there were 70,000 trained nurses and over 100 doctors.
- Decline in traditional 'women's work' as governesses, domestic servants, on the land and in mining.
- Changes in technology and commerce brought about many new clerical and secretarial jobs for women in banking, insurance, the Civil Service and commercial companies.
- By the end of the nineteenth century, five million women earned a wage.

Changing attitudes to family life

- The traditional attitude that a woman's place was in the home was still prevalent.
- However, women gained more independence due to the increased use of birth control.
- Middle-class women began to choose to limit their families, as did working-class women – often because young children were no longer a source of income.

Talking Point ▼

It has been argued that by 1900 the debate over the principle of enfranchising women had largely been won. What obstacles existed which hindered women from gaining the vote at the start of the century?

EXPLAIN HOW THESE LATE NINETEENTH-CENTURY DEVELOPMENTS CONTRIBUTED TO THE INCREASING SUPPORT BY 1900 FOR THE PRINCIPLE OF FEMALE SUFFRAGE

Developing legal and political status of women

- **1839** Wife, on separation from husband, could legally claim custody of children under 7.
- **1857** Divorce, although still difficult, was made possible through the courts.
- **1870** and **1882** Women were allowed to keep money and property after marriage.
- **By 1875** Women ratepayers could be elected to school and Poor Law boards.
- **By 1888** Women were qualified to vote at municipal, county council and county borough elections.

Developments in girls' education

- **1840s onwards** Many women gained a more formal training for the role of teacher/governess.
- **1870** Forster's Education Act provided young children, including girls, with a basic education. (This Act did not apply to Scotland where such legislation was already in place.)
- **1870s and 80s** Educational reform resulted in the emergence of new academic schools for middle-class girls, preparing them for commerce and the professions in addition to their expected role as wives and mothers.
- **1870s** Cambridge and London Universities admitted females.
- **By 1900** Compulsory schooling for boys and girls up to the age of 12.

Challenging History Resource Pack. Text © Liz Petheram; Illustrations © Thomas Nelson & Sons Ltd; Photographs © as listed on page 2; sourced texts on p. 4. Published by Thomas Nelson & Sons Ltd 1999.

Examining the evidence: The Suffragettes

Source A

This was the beginning of a campaign the like of which was never known in England, or, for that matter in any other country. We attended every meeting addressed by Mr Churchill. We heckled him unmercifully; we spoiled his best points by flinging back such obvious retorts that the crowds roared with laughter. We questioned Mr Asquith in Sheffield, Mr Lloyd George in Cheshire, the Prime Minister again in Glasgow, and we interrupted a great many other meetings as well. Always we were violently thrown out and insulted. Often we were painfully bruised and hurt.

What good did it do? We have often been asked that question. For one thing, our heckling campaign made women's suffrage a matter of news – it had never been that before. Now the newspapers were full of us.

On February 19, 1906, occurred the first suffrage procession in London. I think there were between three and four hundred women in that procession, poor working-women from the East End, for the most part, leading the way in which numberless women of every rank were afterwards to follow. My eyes were misty with tears as I saw them, standing in line, holding the simple banners which my daughter Sylvia had decorated, waiting for the word of command. Of course our procession attracted a large crowd of intensely amused spectators.

Those women had followed me to the House of Commons. They had defied the police. They were awake at last. Now they were ready to fight for their own human rights. Our militant movement was established.

Emmeline Pankhurst, My Own Story (1914)

Source C

In the year 1906 there was an immensely large public opinion in favour of woman suffrage. But what good did that do the cause? We called upon the public for a great deal more than sympathy. We called upon it to demand of the Government to yield to public opinion and give women votes. And we declared that we would wage war, not only on all anti-suffrage forces, but on all neutral and non-active forces. Every man with a vote was considered a foe to woman suffrage unless he was prepared to be actively a friend.

Not that we believed that the campaign of education ought to be given up. On the contrary, we knew that education must go on, and in much more vigorous fashion than ever before. The first thing we did was to enter upon a sensational campaign to arouse the public to the importance of woman suffrage, and to interest it in our plans for forcing the Government's hands. I think we can claim that our success in this regard was instant, and that it has proved permanent. From the very first, in those early London days, when we were few in numbers and very poor in purse, we made the public aware of the woman suffrage movement as it had never been before.

E. Pankhurst, My Own Story (1914); quoted in D. Read's Documents from Edwardian England (1973)

Source B

NATIONAL UNION OF WOMEN'S SUFFRAGE SOCIETIES,

25, VICTORIA ST., WESTMINSTER, S.W.

President - - Mrs. HENRY FAWCETT, LL.D.

LEADING FACTS OF THE MOVEMENT

FOR THE

Parliamentary Enfranchisement of Women.

1866 Petition in favour of granting the Parliamentary Franchise to Women, presented to the House of Commons by John Stuart Mill, signed by 1,499 women.

1867 Mr. J. S. Mill's amendment to substitute "person" for "man" in the Representation of the People Act, rejected by a majority of 121.

Women's Suffrage Societies formed in London, Manchester, and Edinburgh.

1868 At General Election 5,000 women in Manchester and many women in other places applied to be placed on the Parliamentary Register; the Court of Common Pleas decided against their claim.

Women's Suffrage Societies formed in Birmingham, Bristol, and many other places.

1869 Full Suffrage granted to the women of Wyoming (U.S.A.).

1873 Memorials from 11,000 women, presented to Mr. Gladstone and Mr. Disraeli, in favour of Women's Suffrage.

1881 Suffrage granted to women in the Isle of Man for the House of Keys.

1888 A memorial signed by 169 Members of Parliament, presented to the First Lord of the Treasury, asking Government to give a day for a Women's Suffrage Bill.

1889 A Protest against Women's Suffrage, signed by 106 women, appeared in the *Nineteenth Century* and called forth in less than a fortnight a counter-declaration in favour, signed by 2,000 women; of these, 600 representative names were published in the *Fortnightly Review*.

1893 Full Suffrage granted to women in New Zealand.

Full Suffrage granted to women in Colorado (U.S.A.).

1894 Full Suffrage granted to women in South Australia.

1895 Equal Suffrage granted to women in Utah (U.S.A.).

was their militancy a hindrance or a help?

Source D

Miss Pankhurst and Miss Kenney, the two ladies whose zeal for women's suffrage led to their being ejected from a Liberal demonstration held in Manchester Free Trade Hall on Friday night, refused to pay the fines which were imposed on Saturday, when they were charged with disorderly behaviour, and are now in Strangeways Gaol.

The prosecution alleged that the two women went to the meeting with the intention of creating a disturbance, shouting and shrieking 'Treat us like men'. When the attendants turned them out they were however anxious to be treated like ladies. Miss Pankhurst was so angered that she spat in the face of a police superintendent, and an inspector, and the latter she struck twice in the mouth.

From the *Daily Mail*, 16 October 1905

PUNCH, OR THE LONDON CHARIVARI.—January 17, 1906.

THE SHRIEKING SISTER.

THE SENSIBLE WOMAN. *"YOU HELP OUR CAUSE? WHY, YOU'RE ITS WORST ENEMY!"*

Punch *cartoon, 1906*

Source E

National Union of Women's Suffrage Societies,
14, GT. SMITH STREET, WESTMINSTER, LONDON, S.W.

LAW-ABIDING   NON-PARTY

President:– Mrs. HENRY FAWCETT, LL.D.

14 REASONS
For Supporting Women's Suffrage.

1.—Because it is the foundation of all political liberty that those who obey the Law should be able to have a voice in choosing those who make the Law.

2.—Because Parliament should be the reflection of the wishes of the people.

3.—Because Parliament cannot fully reflect the wishes of the people when the wishes of women are without any direct representation.

4.—Because most Laws affect women as much as men, and some Laws affect women especially.

5.—Because the Laws which affect women especially are now passed without consulting those persons whom they are intended to benefit.

6.—Because Laws affecting children should be regarded from the woman's point of view as well as the man's.

7.—Because every session questions affecting the home come up for consideration in Parliament.

8.—Because women have experience which should be helpfully brought to bear on domestic legislation.

9.—Because to deprive women of the vote is to lower their position in common estimation.

10.—Because the possession of the vote would increase the sense of responsibility amongst women towards questions of public importance.

11.—Because public-spirited mothers make public-spirited sons.

12.—Because large numbers of intelligent, thoughtful, hardworking women desire the franchise.

13.—Because the objections raised against their having the franchise are based on sentiment, not on reason.

14.—Because – to sum all reasons up in one – it is for the common good of all.

Published by the NATIONAL UNION OF WOMEN'S SUFFRAGE SOCIETIES,
14, Great Smith Street, S.W.: and
Printed by the Templar Printing Works, 168, Edmund Street, Birmingham.

QUESTIONS ON THE SOURCES

1 How did suffragette tactics differ from those of the NUWSS?

2 What evidence is there to support the arguments that:

   (a) suffragettes hindered their own cause?

   (b) suffragette tactics benefited the movement's aims?

What the historians say

Source F

Who or what contributed most to the eventual granting of the franchise to women? The answer that springs most readily to mind concerns the campaigns of Emmeline Pankhurst and her daughters, Christabel and Sylvia, between 1905 and 1914. This is hardly surprising: all movements like to have heroes and martyrs. The images of suffragettes being manhandled by police, undergoing hunger strikes and forcible feeding in prison, and in the case of Emily Wilding Davison, meeting a violent death for the cause, are too indelible to be easily forgotten. Moreover, the Pankhursts possessed a talent for self-publicity which they exercised for years after the campaign had ended.

But history is an unsentimental business, and careful analysis of the activities of the militant suffragettes has gone a long way to exploding the extravagant claims made by their leaders about their role in winning the vote. In particular three qualifications about their significance can be made. First, not only did militant methods fail to shake the government's view on women's suffrage, they actually alienated, if only temporarily, some of the support for the cause as is clear from the shifting pattern of voting in Parliament.

Second, Pankhurst claims to have won over public opinion scarcely seem consistent with the growing hostility shown by the crowds at their meetings, the defeat of their candidate at the Bow and Bromley by-election in 1912, and the deep gulf between them and working-class women. Always a small organisation, the Women's Social and Political Union repeatedly split until it became a mere rump of those who were willing to give unquestioning loyalty to the Pankhursts. Third, during the critical period 1916–1918 when enfranchisement was actually being achieved, the Pankhursts had abandoned their campaign for women and exercised little influence except, perhaps, as a memory; none of them returned to women's causes again.

Martin Pugh, *Women's Suffrage in Britain 1867–1928* (1980)

Source G

However, it is true that later supposedly 'violent' means of militant protest were engaged in, stone-throwing being the first. The decision to eschew deputations and the like in favour of stone-throwing was a result of 'Black Friday', 18 November 1910, and of other incidents when protesting women were met with incredible violence and sexual assault by the police and the public – that is, by *men*. Much better to be arrested quickly after the throwing of a stone or two at a window or car than brave sexual and physical assault of the kind that had led to many injuries and at least three known deaths following Black Friday. However, self protection was not the motive of the women who initiated this new form of militancy…

However, stone-throwing was an action against *property* and not persons – in spite of the way such incidents were described in court by police officers and reported in the press. And usually the stones were wrapped in paper carrying a WSPU message. Con Lytton, for example, describes how she took great care to throw stones as low as possible against official cars to ensure there was no possibility of anyone being hurt by them (Lytton, 1914, pp. 208–12). The firing of pillar-boxes and the later firing or bombing of empty buildings were also not designed to harm people. Of course, it might be objected that burning letters was indirectly harmful. Emily Davison, the initiator of this particular militant act, tried to ensure that it wasn't or that it would hurt only the kind of well-off people who could easily absorb consequent financial losses. This and the secret arson and bombing campaigns will be returned to later.

The NUWSS grew greatly in the period after 1906, as a direct consequence of the WSPU making feminism visible and attractive. In 1906 when the WSPU started in earnest, the NUWSS had 31 branches; in 1909, it had 130; in 1910, the start of 'violent' militancy with stone-throwing, 210; in 1914, 496. Of course, branches can be largely empty; however, membership figures show an increase from 13,161 members in 1909 to 54,592 in 1914.

Ann Morley and Liz Stanley, *The Life and Death of Emily Wilding Davison* (1988)

TASKS

1   How and why do these two historians vary in their interpretation of suffragette militancy?

2   From the primary and secondary sources given and your own research, provide evidence to support the two views:

    (a) suffragette militancy hindered the cause;

    (b) suffragette militancy was a necessary tactic to further the cause.

Talking Point ▼

1   Do militant tactics ever help a pressure group achieve its ultimate aim?

2   What examples can you use to illustrate your opinion?

Preview

By 1914 Ireland was on the brink of civil war – a crisis postponed only by the outbreak of World War I. The Liberal government after 1910 were attempting to pass the third Home Rule Bill, supported by the Irish Nationalist MPs led by John Redmond. As the likelihood of this becoming legislation grew due to the recently curtailed powers of the House of Lords in 1911, those bitterly opposed to Home Rule – the Ulstermen, supported by the Conservative and Unionist Party – took up a stance to prevent Home Rule for Ireland becoming law.

What was the situation in Ireland by 1914?

Source A

GRAVE NEWS FROM IRELAND

The grave news which we publish this morning from the European capitals is accompanied, we are sorry to say, by very serious intelligence from Ireland. An attempt at gun-running by The National Volunteers near Dublin yesterday morning resulted in collisions between the Volunteers, the public, the police and the military. Four persons were killed and some sixty injured, of whom several are not expected to live. The excitement in Dublin is intense.

The Times, 27 July 1914; quoted in Benning (1980);
© Times Newspapers Limited, London 1914,
[Photocopying allowed for classroom use only]

Source B

At the present time two opposing forces, with approximately a total strength of 200,000 men are being systematically and deliberately raised, trained, equipped and organised on a military basis in Ireland.

Secret Army Memorandum to Cabinet, 4 July 1914; quoted in
Butler and Jones's *Britain in the 20th Century Documentary
Reader* (1994)

Talking Point ▼

- How is Ireland governed today?

- How does this differ from the government of Ireland in the nineteenth century?

- When did the division of Ireland occur?

- What problems confront present-day governments in their attempt to solve the Northern Ireland question?

What was Home Rule?

Home Rule would have allowed Ireland a degree of political autonomy. An Irish Parliament was proposed which would have devolved power to deal with internal Irish affairs. Ireland would still elect representatives to Westminster, where issues affecting them such as foreign policy, trade and financial policy were dealt with.

Challenging History Resource Pack. Text © Liz Petheram; Illustrations © Thomas Nelson & Sons Ltd; Photographs © as listed on page 2; sourced texts on p. 4. Published by Thomas Nelson & Sons Ltd 1999.

Why was Ireland heading for Civil War by 1914?

TASKS

1 Using the background notes below, the documents and timeline on the following pages, and your own research, outline the evidenced arguments put forward by each of the four main players in a debate over Home Rule.

2 Prepare a classroom debate on the issue of Home Rule that could take place in the form of the Buckingham Palace Conference, July 1914.

The four key players were as follows:

LIBERAL GOVERNMENT

- Home Rule had been a traditional nineteenth-century Liberal policy. Gladstone had unsuccessfully introduced two Home Rule Bills in 1886 and 1893.
- Liberal policy in 1900 was to maintain the Union of Ireland and Britain through diversity. Peaceful devolution of a degree of power to satisfy nationalist demands was proposed.
- After 1910 Liberals needed the support of Redmond's Irish Nationalist MPs (84) to form a government. Asquith promised Home Rule to Redmond to gain such support.

IRISH NATIONALISTS

- Moderate Parliamentary Party was led by John Redmond who, after the Liberals came to power in 1906, reunited and reinvigorated this group. Redmond's main aims were Home Rule and to fend off the electoral threat from Sinn Fein in Ireland.
- Extreme Nationalists in Ireland were Republican. They aimed for complete Irish independence and saw Home Rule as an unacceptable compromise. Nationalist demands for an end to the Union with England and for a separate Parliament for Ireland had increased during the late nineteenth century. This was encouraged by elected county councils in Ireland (1898), failure of the British government to solve Irish problems, a Gaelic revival, growing disillusionment with their Irish MPs, and in 1905 the founding of Sinn Fein, a pro-independence party, by Arthur Griffiths.

CONSERVATIVE AND UNIONIST PARTY

- Ireland was seen as part of the British Empire. Any concessions to Irish Nationalism would undermine the Empire and have worldwide ramifications.
- Since the first Home Rule Bill (1886), Conservative support was given to Ulster's opposition to Home Rule. They believed a Dublin Parliament with limited powers would inevitably lead to full independence.
- The Conservative majority in the Lords had been used to counter Liberal policy in Ireland. After 1911 this was no longer possible.
- Conservative policy in 1900 was to maintain the Union of Ireland with England.

ULSTER UNIONISTS

- In the nineteenth century the demands of the Protestant Ulstermen in the North (see map on page 29) emerged on the political agenda.
- In Ulster there was a large Protestant community in a mainly Roman Catholic Ireland.
- The North was industrial and prosperous, contrasting with the agricultural and economically backward South.
- Protestant Ulstermen (or Orangemen), because of historic, cultural, religious and economic links with England, firmly supported Union. With the support of the Conservative Party they began to develop political organisations. In 1891 the Irish Unionist Association was formed in Dublin and in 1905 the Ulster Unionist Council was created to bring together Protestant organisations.
- If Home Rule was passed they feared a parliament in Dublin which would be dominated by Catholic and agricultural interests.

Challenging History Resource Pack. Text © Liz Petheram; Illustrations © Thomas Nelson & Sons Ltd; Photographs © as listed on page 2; sourced texts on p. 4. Published by Thomas Nelson & Sons Ltd 1999.

For and against Home Rule

A NATIONALIST VIEW

Source C

Redmond speech on Home Rule, 1907

What we mean by Home Rule is that in the management of all exclusively Irish affairs Irish public opinion shall be as powerful as the public opinion of Canada or Australia is in the management of Canadian or Australian affairs. That is our claim; we rest that claim on historic right, on historic title, but we rest it also on the admitted failure of British government in Ireland for the last 100 years. I say admitted failure. What Unionist or Conservative statesman has gone to Ireland for the last twenty five years to carry out Unionist policy who has not frankly admitted that the state of government in Ireland was injurious to Ireland and impossible to sustain? Why, I myself heard the present Leader of the Unionist Party in the House of Lords declare a few short months ago that the system of government by Dublin Castle was an anachronism and could not continue to exist as it is to-day. What has the history been of your rule? The history of famine, of misery, of insurrection, of depopulation. These are facts that cannot be disputed. There have been three unsuccessful outbreaks of insurrection during that time, there has been one great famine which swept away in one year 1,500,000 of the Irish people by starvation. There have been famines every decade during that period, and depopulation is going on to this very moment, so that in a little over fifty years one half of the population has entirely gone. You may differ from me as to the precise cause of all these things, but you must admit that your rule has not been a success but a failure. We have always been quite frank in these matters in the House of Commons, and I say that if your rule had been as good in the last 100 years as it has been bad, if it had led to the material advancement of Ireland – as in the case of Egypt – still our claim would have remained, because we stand by the principle enunciated by the Prime Minister himself quite recently, when he said, 'good government can never be a substitute for self-government'. No man has any doubt what our demand means, and it can only be met by full trust in the Irish people.

Parliamentary Debates. House of Commons, 5th Series vol. xxxvi col. 1424–6 (1912)

AN ULSTER VIEW

Source D

Ulster's Solemn League and Covenant

Being convinced in our consciences that Home Rule would be disastrous to the material well-being of Ulster, as well as of the whole of Ireland, subversive of our civil and religious freedom, destructive of our citizenship, and perilous to the unity of the Empire, we whose names are underwritten, men of Ulster, loyal subjects of His Gracious Majesty King George V, humbly relying on the God whom our fathers in days of stress and trial confidently trusted, hereby pledge ourselves in solemn Covenant throughout this our time of threatened calamity to stand by one another in defending for ourselves and our children our cherished position of equal citizenship in the United Kingdom, and in using all means which may be found necessary to defeat the present conspiracy to set up a Home Rule Parliament in Ireland; and, in the event of such a Parliament being forced upon us, we further solemnly and mutually pledge ourselves to refuse to recognise its authority. In sure confidence that God will defend the right, we hereto subscribe our names, and, further, we individually declare that we have not already signed this Covenant.

The Times, 30 September 1912; quoted in Butler and Jones' *Britain in the 20th Century Documentary Reader* (1994); © Times Newspapers Limited, London 1912, [Photocopying allowed for classroom use only]

A CONSERVATIVE VIEW

Source E

Balfour speech at Nottingham, 1913

The Irish problem, now that all Irish grievances connected with land, religion, and finance have been removed, is essentially due to the exclusive and often hostile form which Irish patriotism outside Ulster has assumed.

This finds no justification either in differences of race or in the memories of native institutions destroyed by foreign usurpation.

It has its origin in the unhappy circumstances of Irish history, and especially in the inevitable fusion, both in fact and in the memory of the Roman Catholic Irish, of wrongs due to religious divisions with others that followed on the heels of rebellion and civil war.

The memory of these unhappy events was kept alive long after the events were over by the social irritation due to one of the worst systems of land tenure which has ever existed; and though this and all the other causes which have produced the Irish problem are now removed, their effects, as is inevitable, survive them…

For these claims, if they are genuine, can never be satisfied by the Home Rule Bill; and if that Bill were really to put an end to the Nationalist agitation, it would be conclusive proof that the agitation was factitious, and that the cause of Irish patriotism in its exclusive form was already lost.

But if Home Rule cannot really satisfy Nationalist aspirations, from every other point of view it stands condemned. Financially, administratively, and constitutionally, it is indefensible; and considered from these points of view few indeed are the Home Rulers who sincerely attempt to defend it.

Opinions and Argument from Speeches and Addresses of the Earl of Balfour (1927)

Challenging History Resource Pack. Text © Liz Petheram; Illustrations © Thomas Nelson & Sons Ltd; Photographs © as listed on page 2; sourced texts on p. 4. Published by Thomas Nelson & Sons Ltd 1999.

Home Rule

CRISIS YEARS	FOR		AGAINST	
	Liberal Government	**Nationalists**	**Ulster Unionists**	**Conservative and Unionist Party**
1910	January – General Election, Liberals gained 275 seats. April – Budget passed with Irish and Labour support. December – General Election, both Liberal and Conservatives 272 seats. Liberals used Irish support (84) to form government.	Support for Lloyd George's budget in return for Liberals curbing power of Lords and introducing Home Rule.	Sir Edward Carson, Irish Unionist MP and lawyer, elected as Leader.	January – 273 MPs returned. December – 272 MPs returned (exactly same as Liberals).
1911	August – Parliament Bill passed on condition from Redmond that Home Rule be introduced. Home Rule becomes a government priority.	Redmond exploits his advantage of a hung Parliament and wins Liberal promise to introduce Home Rule.	September – Craigavon – a mass demonstration to show hostility to Home Rule. Plans to form separate government for Ulster.	Bonar Law leads Conservative support for Ulster. Conservative-dominated House of Lords loses power and Conservative Party loses a useful tool whilst in opposition.
1912	April – third Home Rule Bill • Establish two-chamber Irish Parliament. • Irish Parliament to deal with internal affairs. • 42 Irish MPs at Westminster. • Central government was to have control over foreign policy, trade and taxation. Asquith refused concessions to Ulster.	Support for Home Rule through House of Commons.	February – hostile Protestant reaction to Churchill's attendance at Belfast Ulster Hall; meeting re-sited to Celtic Park. September – 'Ulster Day'. Ulster Covenant declared.	Easter – Bonar Law visits Belfast. July – rally at Blenheim Palace to demonstrate support for Ulster.
1913	January – Lords reject Home Rule 326–69. July – Lords again reject Home Rule, meaning Bill will become law after one more passage through Commons. Asquith seeks compromise in the different groups. Government steps up military in Ireland.	Extreme Nationalists make preparations to further their cause. Irish volunteers constituted. Irish Republican Brotherhood and Sinn Fein – both make preparations for confrontation. Redmond – against violence but failed to curb Irish Nationalist activity.	January – Ulster Volunteer Force established. Ulster Rifle Clubs and Lodges of Orange Order spread over Northern Ireland. Tension heightens as Home Rule becomes an inevitability.	Conservatives claim that Home Rule is being pursued unconstitutionally as it does not have a mandate from the electorate. It was not the issue they voted on in 1910.
1914	March – problem of 'Curragh Mutiny'. Introduction of Amending Bill, giving Ulster counties six years to opt out, failed to stem crisis.	Military build-up.	Military build-up. April – UVF gunrunning at Larne, Bangor and Donaghadee.	March – British Covenant organised by the Union Defence League – 2 million signed. Funds raised for arms for Ulster

July ◄———————————— BUCKINGHAM PALACE CONFERENCE ————————————►

August ◄——————————————————— WORLD WAR I ———————————————————►

Challenging History Resource Pack. Text © Liz Petheram; Illustrations © Thomas Nelson & Sons Ltd; Photographs © as listed on page 2; sourced texts on p. 4. Published by Thomas Nelson & Sons Ltd 1999.

FROM ISOLATION TO WORLD CONFLICT, BRITISH FOREIGN POLICY 1900–14

Preview

Within the 14 years from 1900 to 1914, Britain's foreign policy transformed dramatically from:

- 'splendid isolation'
- to no alliances or close diplomatic commitments
- to a major power involved in World War I.

How and why did this three-stage transformation occur? Decisions in foreign policy were in the hands of an expert elite at the Foreign Office led by Foreign Secretaries Lord Lansdowne during the Conservative government to 1906 and Sir Edward Grey during the Liberal government up to 1914. The conduct of foreign policy was crucial both for Britain's international position and also because it impacted on government spending, leading to difficult decisions between defence expenditure and social reform.

Timeline to War

pre-1900	Triple Alliance
	Franco-Russian Alliance
1900	Lord Lansdowne, Foreign Secretary
1901	Agreement with USA
1902	End of Boer War
	Alliance with Japan
1903	
1904	Russo-Japanese War
	Anglo-French Entente
1905	Moroccan crisis
1906	Sir Edward Grey, Foreign Secretary
1907	Anglo-Russian Convention
1908	Bosnian crisis
1909	
1910	
1911	Agadir crisis
1912	1st Balkan War
1913	2nd Balkan War
1914	Assassination at Sarajevo
	Outbreak of World War I

Talking Point ▼

1 Why was there increasing unease in Britain by 1900?

2 Do you agree with many contemporaries that safety lay not in isolation but in alliance?

3 Where were the key trouble spots at that time?

From isolation to conflict – three stages

STAGE ONE:
Britain emerges from isolation

HOW?

USA	– Hay-Pauncefote Treaty	– 1901
JAPAN	– Anglo-Japanese Alliance	– 1902
FRANCE	– Anglo-French Entente	– 1904
RUSSIA	– Anglo-Russian Convention	– 1907

WHY?

❶ Existence of the Triple Alliance between Austria-Hungary, Germany and Italy.

❷ Economic challenge to Britain's prominence from the USA, Japan and Germany.

❸ Universal unpopularity of Britain at the beginning of the twentieth century as a result of colonial disputes with France, Germany and the USA and widespread European support for the Boers in the Boer War.

❹ Imperial Russia's ambitions to expand to China had implications for British trade in the Far East.

❺ Franco-Russian Alliance, 1892, was seen to alter the balance of power.

❻ Increasing military, colonial and economic rivalry of Imperial Germany under Kaiser Wilhelm II and failure to secure an Anglo-German alliance.

Challenging History Resource Pack. Text © Liz Petheram; Illustrations © Thomas Nelson & Sons Ltd; Photographs © as listed on page 2; sourced texts on p. 4. Published by Thomas Nelson & Sons Ltd 1999.

STAGE TWO:

Britain's growing European involvement 1907–14

The existence of two European power blocs

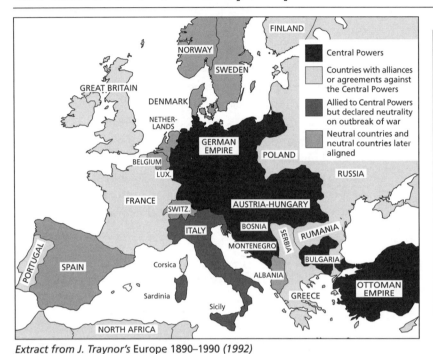

Extract from J. Traynor's Europe 1890–1990 *(1992)*

TASKS

1 Explain how each of the factors below led Britain into increased involvement in Europe in this period:

- European power blocs
- Anglo-German naval race
- Moroccan crisis 1905–06
- Balkan Wars

2 Identify long- and medium-term causes leading to the outbreak of war in 1914 – use pages 33 to 35 and your own research.

North Africa 1905–06 Moroccan crisis

Partridge, 1905, reproduced by permission of the proprietors of Punch

Source A

If there is war between France and Germany it will be very difficult for us to keep out of it. The *Entente* and still more the constant and emphatic demonstrations of affection (official, naval, political, commercial, Municipal and in the Press), have created in France a belief that we should support her in war. The last report from our naval attaché at Toulon said that all the French officers took this for granted... If this expectation is disappointed the French will never forgive us.

Sir Edward Grey, memorandum on Franco–German tension in Morocco, 20 February 1906 (in G.P. Gooch and Harold Temperley (eds) *British Documents on the Origins of the War, 1898–1914*, Vol. III: *The Testing of the Entente, 1904–1906* (1928)

QUESTIONS ON THE SOURCES

1 What was the Moroccan crisis of 1905–06?

2 What was the significance of this crisis to the Anglo-French entente?

3 How does the cartoonist portray his message?

4 What seems to be the motivation behind Grey's argument?

Challenging History Resource Pack. Text © Liz Petheram; Illustrations © Thomas Nelson & Sons Ltd; Photographs © as listed on page 2; sourced texts on p. 4. Published by Thomas Nelson & Sons Ltd 1999.

Anglo-German naval race

Source B

We're a maritime nation – we've grown by the sea and live by it; if we lose command of it we starve. We're unique in that way, just as our huge empire, only linked by the sea, is unique. And yet, read Brassey, Dilke, and those 'Naval Annuals', and see what mountains of apathy and conceit have had to be tackled. It's not the people's fault. We've been safe so long, and grown so rich, that we've forgotten what we owe it to. But there's no excuse for those blockheads of statesmen, as they call themselves, who are paid to see things as they are…

'We're improving, aren't we?'

'Oh, of course, we are! But it's a constant uphill fight; and we aren't ready.' . . . This is only a sample of many similar conversations that we afterwards held, always culminating in the burning question of Germany.

Erskine Childers, *The Riddle of the Sands* (1903) – an early spy novel which warned of British vulnerability to the growing German navy. (1978 edition)

Dreadnought-class ships completed

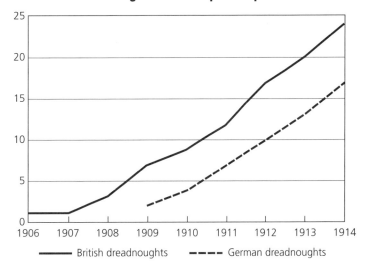

The Anglo-German naval race, 1906–14 (derived from Fleets (Great Britain and Foreign Countries). *Return 113, PP LIV, 1914*

TASK

Find out more about the German and British naval and military build-up during this period.

 The Balkans 1912–14

The Balkans by the end of 1913

The changed face of the Balkans by 1914

Extract from T. Howarth's 20th Century History: The World Since 1900

TASKS

1 From the maps identify how the Balkans changed over these two years and the significance of these alterations.

2 Why did the 1st and 2nd Balkan Wars break out?

3 What was the significance of the Treaty of London 1912 and the Treaty of Bucharest 1913?

STAGE THREE:

1914: crisis year – Britain declares war on Germany

The July crisis

Source C

Sunday 28 June 1914

The month of June was coming to a glorious conclusion. All over Europe people were basking under a prolonged heatwave which showed no sign of coming to an end. Prospects for the summer were superb. Although the season had only just begun, seaside towns were already crowded with visitors, many eager to display the latest daring fashions in below-the-knee swimwear. In the leafy suburb of Wimbledon the groundsmen spent all of Sunday watering the courts in preparation for the lawn tennis championships which were due to resume the next day. Meanwhile, butlers and manservants across the continent put the finishing touches to their employers' traditional routine of hunting expeditions, holidays, spas and cures which characterised the summer months. In Germany, Kaiser William II had left behind weighty matters of state, donned his sailing outfit and spent the day under the blazing sun racing his yacht *Meteor* at Kiel.

Meanwhile, several hundred miles to the south, Archduke Franz Ferdinand – heir to the throne of Austria-Hungary – was spending his wedding anniversary with his wife, Countess Sophie, on a state visit to Sarajevo. They received a very warm welcome and the glorious weather enabled them to drive through the crowded streets in an open-topped car. However, Sarajevo was the capital of the former Turkish province of Bosnia, a state inhabited by Slavs but occupied since 1908 by the Austro-Hungarian Empire. A south Slav terrorist organisation consisting of ultra-nationalist officers and student intellectuals (calling itself the 'Black Hand' gang) regarded the Austrian prince as the figurehead of an occupying empire which stood in the way of Slav independence. At the centre of this radical group, and beyond the direct control of the Serbian government, was Gavrillo Princip, who had decided to lead an assassination attempt against the Austrian prince.

The bungling nature of these amateur assassins meant that two attempts on the Heir Apparent's life were necessary. After a hand grenade had missed its intended target but injured 20 onlookers, officials decided that the visit should be cut short and the route home changed. In retrospect, one of the most startling aspects of that fateful day in Sarajevo is that the authorities were unable to guarantee Franz Ferdinand's safety after the first assassination attempt had failed. Crucially, the driver of the first vehicle in the four-car entourage did not follow the fresh instructions and made a right turn back along the original route. It was only when the second car, containing the royal couple had followed suit that officials shouted out instructions to stop and turn back. As the driver of Franz Ferdinand's car tried in vain to find reverse gear, Princip stepped out of the crowd and onto the running board. With his victim helpless and within a few feet, Princip almost lost his nerve. The sight of Countess Sophie made him hesitate but then nationalism overcame chivalry and at point-blank range he fired several shots. A few minutes later the couple were dead.

John Traynor, *Europe 1890–1990* (1992)

TASK

Research further the role of Sir Edward Grey during this period 1906–14.
Find arguments to defend and attack the decisions he took.

QUESTIONS ON THE SOURCES

1   Explain why the Serbian, Gavrillo Princip assassinated Archduke Franz Ferdinand in Sarajevo.

2   Why did this event, described by Traynor as 'an isolated act of terrorism in an area of which few Europeans had ever heard', trigger a European-wide political crisis throughout July?

3   What policy did Sir Edward Grey follow during this critical period?

The August crisis

PUNCH, OR THE LONDON CHARIVARI.—October 21, 1914.

UNCONQUERABLE.

THE KAISER. "SO YOU SEE—YOU'VE LOST EVERYTHING."
THE KING OF THE BELGIANS. "NOT MY SOUL."

Partridge, 1914, reproduced by permission of the proprietors of Punch

QUESTIONS ON THE SOURCES

1   What attitudes are conveyed by the cartoonist?

2   Why did the Germans' invasion of Belgium precipitate Britain's declaration of war on 4 August 1914?

Challenging History Resource Pack. Text © Liz Petheram; Illustrations © Thomas Nelson & Sons Ltd; Photographs © as listed on page 2; sourced texts on p. 4. Published by Thomas Nelson & Sons Ltd 1999.

FROM LIBERALISM TO LABOUR 1900–18:
THE DEBATE, PART I

Preview

In 1906 the Liberal Party was triumphantly returned to power with 400 seats, a landslide majority which brought to an end over a decade of Conservative rule. Yet only four years later the 1910 election was to prove the last occasion on which a Liberal government was formed in Britain. In 1924 the Labour Party established its first administration, albeit a minority, and by 1929 it was clearly the alternative to the Conservative Party in a system dominated by two parties. The Liberal Party gained only 40 seats in 1924 and 59 seats in 1929. The Conservative and the Labour parties have remained the two contenders for power throughout the rest of the twentieth century.

A debate amongst historians has arisen over explanations of this transformation in the British political system. Interpretations fall into two broad categories – from a Liberal point of view:

1 OPTIMISTIC

- Liberalism adapted well to twentieth-century class-based politics and the necessity to appeal to the working-class electorate.

- Although the Liberal government before World War I encountered problems, they were addressed with a degree of success.

- The Labour Party pre-1914 had many problems and were of little threat to the Liberals.

- The decline of Liberalism came as a result of several factors after 1914, such as the impact of world war and the extension of the franchise in 1918.

2 PESSIMISTIC

- Liberalism, in terms both of philosophy and practical party considerations, was fundamentally weak by the twentieth century. These weaknesses were illustrated and in fact worsened by problems which beset the pre-war government.

- The development of class-based politics, together with the emergence of the Labour Party solely representing working-class interests, caused the inevitable decline of the Liberal Party before 1914 and its subsequent replacement by the Labour Party in the 1920s.

Three main questions need to be examined:
- How strong was the Liberal Party before 1914?
- Was the Labour Party a threat to the Liberals before 1914?
- How significant was World War I in the decline of Liberalism?

ELECTION RESULTS OF LIBERALS AND LABOUR

	Libs	Lab
1900	184	2
1906	400	29
1910 (Jan)	275	40
1910 (Dec)	272	42
1918	133 (coalition Liberals) 28 (independent Libs)	63
1922	54	142
1924	40	151

Talking Point ▼

Look at the number of MPs for both parties from 1900 to 1924. What do the figures suggest?

Challenging History Resource Pack. Text © Liz Petheram; Illustrations © Thomas Nelson & Sons Ltd; Photographs © as listed on page 2; sourced texts on p. 4. Published by Thomas Nelson & Sons Ltd 1999.

How strong was the Liberal Party before 1914?

What the historians say

Source A

Thus the first quarter of the twentieth century saw two sorts of change in British politics. The first sort centred upon the emergence of class politics in a stable form; the second sort upon the effective replacement of the Liberal Party by the Labour Party. But the first does not in any simple way explain the second. For one thing, the chronology is wrong. By 1910, the change to class politics was substantially complete. That from Liberalism to Labour had not really begun. It was not a light thing to overturn one party and make another to put in its place. At the beginning of the second decade of the twentieth century it looked as though both Labour and Liberalism would be subsumed in progressivism. It seemed that social democracy in England was bound up with the prospects of the Liberal Party; and in the generation after its downfall the social democratic record is not one of achievement.

P.F. Clarke, *Lancashire and the New Liberalism* (1971)

Source B

Thus, the best efforts of Liberal statesmanship to prepare the party to appeal more effectively to a working-class electorate in an era of class politics seemed to be failing. Neither the new liberalism nor Liberal policies of social reform represented a fundamental reorientation of the Liberal Party so that it could represent the interests of the working class rather than those of middle-class Nonconformists. The progressive alliance offered no solution to containing the challenge of Labour for the allegiance of the working-class voter. If class politics were coming, so was the decline of the Liberal Party – not imminently, perhaps, but eventually and inevitably.

G.L. Bernstein, *Liberalism and Liberal Politics in Edwardian England* (1986)

Source C

The majority of people did not think in economics then, but in politics. In 1910, an industrious man might still believe that he had a chance of improving himself, and that his children and his grandchildren would climb higher rather than descend as the years went on. And yet that smothering security… had to be overthrown; it was the very essence of Victorian respectability, and the ultimate expression of it was parliamentary mediation. The workers did not want to be safe any more; they wanted to live, to take chances, to throw caution to the winds; they had been repressed too long. And so the deepest impulse in the great strike movement of 1910–14 was an unconscious one, an enormous energy pressing up from the depths of the soul; and Parliament shuddered before it and under its impact Liberal England died.

G. Dangerfield, *The Strange Death of Liberal England* (1936)

Source D

The present author's *Political Change and the Labour Party 1900–18* (Cambridge University Press, publication March 1990) is unprecedented because it combines new ideas on the analysis of political and electoral change with extensive research into every aspect of the existing debate. The book reassesses the ideological, political, organisational and electoral strengths and weaknesses of the Edwardian Liberal and Labour parties. It is argued that the Liberal Party's success was not founded solely on New Liberal ideas and class politics, but on an ability to mobilise working-class votes while retaining some middle-class support and an additional base in rural areas and market towns. This achievement was unrivalled until 1945. Yet the party was not without weaknesses. In particular, Labour was stronger than the Liberals in areas where specific social, occupational and political circumstances prevailed. This base, growing before 1914, was expanded by wartime events which considerably increased Labour's credibility with voters in these areas. Elsewhere, the Liberals were only defeated so completely at the 1918 election because of the chaotic nature of their position and because of their attitude to the war.

The book rejects the idea that Labour would inevitably become the sole anti-Tory party. It shows how a three-party system was developing, and explains why Labour emerged – against the political trends – as the dominant anti-Tory force in British politics. Labour's expansion cannot be explained by social changes. Policies and political images which varied according to local circumstances, and combined with particular local conditions, were equally important.

D. Tanner, 'The Rise of the Labour Party', from *Modern History Review* (November 1989)

QUESTIONS ON THE SOURCES

1 How does each of these historians view the state of the Liberal Party by 1914?

2 Can you deduce from these extracts any indications as to historians' time of writing, evidence and approach? In what ways might these considerations affect their interpretations?

Examining the evidence

Source 1

What then is the matter with the Liberals? For fifty years, in the middle of the last century, we may recognise their party as 'a great instrument of progress', wrenching away the shackles – political, fiscal, legal, theological and social – that hindered individual advancement. The shackles are by no means wholly got rid of, but the political force of this Old Liberalism is spent. During the last twenty years its aspirations and its watchwords, its ideas of daily life and its conceptions of the universe, have become increasingly distasteful to the ordinary citizen as he renews his youth from generation to generation. Its worship of individual liberty evokes no enthusiasm. Its reliance on 'freedom of contract' and 'supply and demand', with its corresponding 'voluntaryism' in religion and philanthropy, now seems to work out disastrously for the masses, who are too poor to have what the economists call an 'effective demand' for even the minimum conditions of physical and mental health necessary to national well-being. Its very admiration for that favourite Fenian abstraction, the 'principle of nationality', now appears to us as but Individualism writ large, being, in truth, the assertion that each distinct race, merely because it thinks itself a distinct race (which it never is, by the way), has an inherent right to have its own government, and work out its own policy, unfettered by any consideration of the effect of this independence on other races, or on the world at large.

Of all this the rising generations of voters are deadly tired. When they hear the leading Liberal debater shouting the Liberal war cry of fifty years ago, 'Peace, Retrenchment and Reform,' and explaining it as a claim for absolute quiescence in Downing Street, with the Treasury cutting down all expenditure, and the Cabinet doing nothing but tinker with the electoral machinery, what can they say but 'You are old, Father William'?

Sidney Webb, 'Lord Rosebery's Escape from Houndsditch', *The Nineteenth Century* (September 1901) quoted in Morgan (1971)

QUESTIONS ON THE SOURCES

1 According to Sidney Webb in 1901:
   (a) what did nineteenth-century Liberalism achieve?
   (b) what were the main tenets of this Old Gladstonian Liberalism?

2 Explain the meaning of 'You are old, Father William'.

Source 2

While these curious changes have been occupying the attention of the party works, a not less important modification has been consummated in the internal conception of the Liberal Party. It has not abandoned in any respect its historic championship of Liberty, in all its forms under every sky; but it has become acutely conscious of the fact that political freedom, however precious, is utterly incomplete without a measure at least of social and economic independence. This realisation is not confined to our islands. It is taking hold of men's minds as it never has before, in every popularly governed State. All over the world the lines of cleavage are ceasing to be purely political, and are becoming social and economic. The present majority in the House of Commons is pervaded by a social spirit, which is all the more lively and earnest because it has yet to find clear-cut and logical formularies of articulate expression. A great body of opinion is slowly moving forward, conscious of possessing in its midst a vital truth, conscious, too, of the almost superhuman difficulty of affording to it any definition at once sufficiently comprehensive and precise. It is for this reason that no hard and fast line can be drawn between the varied elements which constitute the strength of the present Government upon any ground of political theory.

It is certain that as we enter upon these untrodden fields of British politics we shall need the aid of every moral and religious force which is alive in England to-day. Sacrifices will be required from every class in the population; the rich must contribute in money and the poor in service, if their children are to tread a gentler path towards a fairer goal. A fiscal system which prudently but increasingly imposes the necessary burdens of the State upon unearned wealth will not only be found capable of providing the funds which will be needed, but will also stimulate enterprise and production. And thus from many quarters we may work towards the establishment of that Minimum Standard below which competition cannot be allowed, but above which it may continue healthy and free, to vivify and fertilise the world. It is because the influence of *The Nation* may be powerful to aid and further these causes, that I send you my good wishes and congratulations to-day. – I am, Sir,

Yours faithfully,
Winston S. Churchill.

W.S. Churchill, 'The Untrodden field of Politics' from *The Nation* (7 March 1908) quoted in Morgan (1971)

QUESTIONS ON THE SOURCES

1 According to Churchill in 1908, what was now considered essential to the concept of personal liberty?

2 What is he referring to by:
   (a) 'these untrodden fields of British politics'?
   (b) 'that Minimum Standard below which competition cannot be allowed'?

3 What fiscal changes does he propose in order to establish this minimum standard?

TASK

To what extent do primary sources 1 and 2 support the interpretations of Clarke, Bernstein, Dangerfield and Tanner?

Challenging History Resource Pack. Text © Liz Petheram; Illustrations © Thomas Nelson & Sons Ltd; Photographs © as listed on page 2; sourced texts on p. 4. Published by Thomas Nelson & Sons Ltd 1999.

Was the Liberal Party in irreversible decline before 1914?

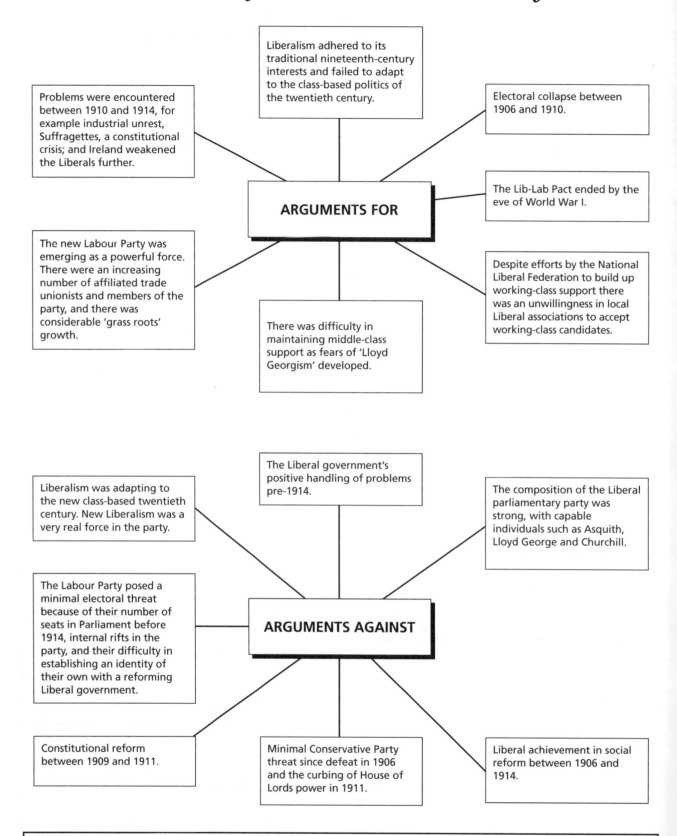

Liberalism adhered to its traditional nineteenth-century interests and failed to adapt to the class-based politics of the twentieth century.

Problems were encountered between 1910 and 1914, for example industrial unrest, Suffragettes, a constitutional crisis; and Ireland weakened the Liberals further.

Electoral collapse between 1906 and 1910.

ARGUMENTS FOR

The Lib-Lab Pact ended by the eve of World War I.

The new Labour Party was emerging as a powerful force. There were an increasing number of affiliated trade unionists and members of the party, and there was considerable 'grass roots' growth.

Despite efforts by the National Liberal Federation to build up working-class support there was an unwillingness in local Liberal associations to accept working-class candidates.

There was difficulty in maintaining middle-class support as fears of 'Lloyd Georgism' developed.

The Liberal government's positive handling of problems pre-1914.

Liberalism was adapting to the new class-based twentieth century. New Liberalism was a very real force in the party.

The composition of the Liberal parliamentary party was strong, with capable individuals such as Asquith, Lloyd George and Churchill.

The Labour Party posed a minimal electoral threat because of their number of seats in Parliament before 1914, internal rifts in the party, and their difficulty in establishing an identity of their own with a reforming Liberal government.

ARGUMENTS AGAINST

Constitutional reform between 1909 and 1911.

Minimal Conservative Party threat since defeat in 1906 and the curbing of House of Lords power in 1911.

Liberal achievement in social reform between 1906 and 1914.

TASK

Research further the evidence which supports these two interpretations.

Which case do you find more convincing? Explain why.

Essay Write a balanced analytical essay which supports your conclusion on whether the Liberal Party were in irreversible decline before 1914.

Challenging History Resource Pack. Text © Liz Petheram; Illustrations © Thomas Nelson & Sons Ltd; Photographs © as listed on page 2; sourced texts on p. 4. Published by Thomas Nelson & Sons Ltd 1999.

FROM LIBERALISM TO LABOUR 1900–18:
THE DEBATE, PART II

Was the Labour Party a threat to the Liberals before 1914?

What the historians say

Source A

It is easy to criticise the Labour Party of the 1910–14 period. Its MPs were divided in their views on a number of important issues – most notably National Insurance – and they could hardly impress the observer of the parliamentary scene.

Yet the difference between the Labour Party and other political parties was that its principal strength lay in its extra-parliamentary organisation, and in this period that organisation was constantly strengthened. Between 1906 and 1914 the number of affiliated trade union members rose from 904,496 to 1,575,391, with a consequent improvement of party funds. If this very largely reflects the growth of trade unionism in the country, the actual expansion of political influence is exemplified by the increase in the number of affiliated trades councils and local Labour Parties, which rose from 73 in 1905/6 to 177 in 1914. The number of persons elected as Labour members of local government and authorities advanced from 56 in the year 1907 to 184 in 1914.

These developments occurred in spite of the concurrent development of interest in the ideas of Syndicalism and direct action, rather than parliamentary methods. There is no real evidence that the 'labour unrest' of these years weakened the performance of the Labour Party in elections; and it is clear that the party's strength was increasing precisely among those workers whose younger militants had taken up with Syndicalism – the South Wales miners and the railwaymen. Among the workers who were not Syndicalists nor even Socialists – and they were still by far the majority – a sort of undogmatic 'Labourism' was establishing itself, which consisted in little more than the opinion that the Labour Party, and not the Liberal, was the party for working men to belong to. This was of course particularly the case now with the miners, whose political solidarity was unmatched by other occupational groups.

H. Pelling, 'Labour and the Downfall of Liberalism' from *Popular Politics and Society in Late Victorian Britain* (1968)

Source B

The years after 1906 were difficult ones for the Labour party. The very magnitude of its success at the election of that year created expectations among its supporters which it could not fulfil, and the objectives which it had set itself were found to be in conflict. Labour wanted to establish its own political identity, to champion its own causes and policies. It also wanted to sustain its growth and organisational expansion. But the policies which it approved could only be effected if they were taken up by the Liberal government, which had won a commanding parliamentary majority in 1906; so that the more effective Labour became as a political pressure group, the more it would seem dependent upon the Liberals. Much the same was true of its prospects of growth. The new party had already benefited from a covert understanding with its radical counterpart. Its further advance seemed to rely upon the co-operation of the Liberals, but the latter would clearly not be willing simply to withdraw from more and more seats. On the other hand, if Labour sought to compete with the Liberals on a wide electoral front, the latter would fight back, and endanger the seats which it already held…

The electoral situation of the party grew no more satisfactory in the years up to 1914. Where it presented candidates at parliamentary by-elections, they were invariably opposed and worsted by the nominees of the two major parties. Yet more discouraging, Labour itself lost seats, particularly in the traditional Liberal coalfields of the Midlands, which the Liberals themselves showed a wish to reclaim. By the outbreak of the war, the size of the parliamentary party had declined from 42 in December 1910 to 37. Since the affiliation of the miners, seven Labour members had been defeated at general elections and by-elections, and one had resigned from the party rather than submit to the relinquishment of his associations with Liberalism, on which his union now insisted.

G. Phillips, *The Rise of the Labour Party* (1992)

QUESTIONS ON THE SOURCES

1   What is Pelling's interpretation of Labour Party strength before 1914 and what evidence does he use to support this argument?

2   What is Phillips's view of the position of the Labour Party between 1906 and 1914, and what evidence supports his argument?

3   Why do these two historians differ in their views?

Examining the evidence

Source 1

10 years ago the vision of the nation was streaked with blood and its mind inflamed by the mad passion of war. Those were dark days for our cause. Unemployment, Old Age Pensions, the sweated woman and the starving child had no place in the thoughts of legislators. No party dare make appeal to the people without profession of at least lip sympathy with the cause of social reform. During these 10 years we have seen an almost revolutionary change in the outlook of the politician on the question of social progress and we are entitled to claim that no small share of the credit for this is due to the presence of our Party in the House of Commons.

Report of the 10th Annual Conference of the Labour Party (February 1910) quoted in J. Hare, J. Boughton and A. Vinson 'The Transformation of the Two-party system' in *From Liberalism to Labour 1900–1924*, HiDES

Source 2

(30 November 1910)… The big thing that has happened in the past two years is that Lloyd George and Winston Churchill have practically taken the *limelight*, not merely from their own colleagues, but from the Labour Party. They stand out as the most advanced politicians. And, if we get a Liberal majority and payment of members, we shall have any number of young Fabians rushing from Parliament, fully equipped for the fray – better than the Labour men – and enrolling themselves behind the two Radical leaders.

Beatrice Webb, *Our Partnership*, eds. B. Drake and M.I. Cole (1948), HiDES

Source 3

We attended the Gala days of the ILP conference as fraternal delegates from the Fabian Society, and listened to endless self-congratulatory speeches from ILP leaders. When the conference settled down to business the ILP leaders were painfully at variance. J. R. MacDonald seems almost preparing for his exit from the ILP. I think he would welcome a really conclusive reason for joining the Liberal Party. Snowden is ill, some say very ill, at once bitter and apathetic; Keir Hardie is 'used up', with no real faith left in the Labour Movement as a revolutionary force. The rank and file are puzzled and disheartened and some of the delegates were seen to be weeping when Snowden fiercely attacked his colleagues in the Parliamentary Labour Party. The cold truth is that the Labour Members have utterly failed to impress the House of Commons and the constituencies as a live force, and have lost confidence in themselves and each other.

Beatrice Webb's Diaries, 1912–1914 (1952) – entry for Summer 1914, HiDES

Source 4

During 1902–1903 3 by-elections took place which greatly improved the position of the movement…The striking electoral victory at Clitheroe was followed next year by successes in 2 by-elections at Woolwich and Barnard Castle. Mr Will Crooks was selected to contest the by-election at Woolwich which he won by converting a previous Tory majority of 2,800 into a Labour majority of 3,200. Six months after this victory at Woolwich a vacancy occurred in Barnard Castle, Division of Durham, which gave Labour its first victory in a 3 cornered contest…

The emergence from the election of 1906 of an Independent Labour Party 29 strong in the House of Commons caused the easy going politicians of the old school who had complacently imagined that politics would for ever continue to be a game of ins and outs between Liberals and Tories, to wake up and begin to take notice.

Philip Snowden, *An Autobiography*, 2 vols (1934), HiDES

QUESTIONS ON THE SOURCES

1   What do these sources tell us of the Labour Party before 1914?

2   Explain why there are contradictions in these sources.

3   To what extent do primary sources 1, 2, 3 and 4 support Pelling's and Phillips's interpretations?

How significant was World War I to the decline of Liberalism?

What the historians say

Source C

To make clear the view taken here about when the Liberal party reached the point of no return, it may be permissible to resort to allegory. The Liberal party can be compared to an individual who, after a period of robust health and great exertion, experienced symptoms of illness (Ireland, Labour unrest, the suffragettes). Before a thorough diagnosis could be made, he was involved in an encounter with a rampant omnibus (the First World War) which mounted the pavement and ran him over. After lingering painfully, he expired. A controversy has existed ever since as to what killed him. One medical school argues that even without the bus he would soon have died; the intimations of illness were symptoms of a grave disease which would shortly have ended his life. Another school goes further, and says the encounter with the bus would not have proved fatal had not the victim's health already been seriously impaired. Neither of these views is accepted here. The evidence for them is insufficient because the ailments had not reached the stage where the ultimate effect could be known. How long, apart from the accident, the victim would have survived, what future (if any) he possessed, cannot be said. All that is known is that at one moment he was up and walking, and at the next he was flat on his back, never to rise again; and in this interval he had been run over by a bus. If it is guesswork to say that the bus was mainly responsible for his demise, it is the most warrantable guess that can be made.

T. Wilson, *Downfall of the Liberal Party* (1966)

Source D

The more the Edwardian evidence underlines the fact that the Liberals were in no imminent danger of decline, let alone eclipse, the more importance must, apparently, be attached to the First World War as the decisive factor in their downfall. Yet while a chronological explanation of this kind may be basically sound it surely cannot be made to run too far; for the war in no sense constitutes a sufficient cause, taken in isolation, for the dramatic disruption of the 1914–26 period. Indeed, the impact of wartime can best be understood in relation to pre-war problems; for the seeds of Liberal decline, patently present before 1914, developed mightily in the conditions of 1914–18.

What were the pre-war sources of weakness? Plainly the Progressive Strategy tended to falter at the point where local activists came under pressure from parliamentary leaders; thus any growing apart of the two such as began to occur after August 1914 was bound to be dangerous. Moreover, success hinged upon the Liberals remaining in office and delivering the full range of radical demands; the wartime collusion with the Conservatives from 1915, loss of office and of the radical initiative spelt disaster. In addition there were at least three areas of policy in which the pre-1914 Liberal government stood in danger of cutting itself off from its traditions: in each case they concerned not the social-economic purposes of Liberalism but its political–moral objectives, and in each case war fostered the conditions in which Labour could uphold these traditional Liberal causes.

M. Pugh, *The Making of Modern British Politics* (1982)

QUESTIONS ON THE SOURCES

1 According to Wilson, what can we infer about the state of the pre-war Liberal Party?

2 To what extent does Pugh agree with Wilson on the impact of World War I on the Liberal Party?

TASK

From your own research, in what ways did World War I damage the Liberal Party and benefit the Labour Party?

Challenging History Resource Pack. Text © Liz Petheram; Illustrations © Thomas Nelson & Sons Ltd; Photographs © as listed on page 2; sourced texts on p. 4. Published by Thomas Nelson & Sons Ltd 1999.

The impact of World War I on the Liberal and Labour Parties

Examining the evidence

Source 5

> Do you feel as much stirred as I do about the wickedness and folly and shame of introducing compulsory service? I feel that this, with Protection, the censorship and a military bureaucracy would make England no place for people like me…
>
> I am enjoying a little rest at this delightful place and am not sorry to see the organised hypocrisy of Liberal Imperialism based upon the unholy alliance of jingoism with socialism falling to pieces…
>
> P.S. Why should all of us Britons be ruined because a little group of Liberal and Tory Imperialists has taken the idiotic resolution of destroying the German nation?

Francis Hirst, editor of the *Economist*, to C.P. Scott,
21 May 1915, from *C.P. Scott Diaries 1911–28*
ed. Trevor Wilson (1970), Collins, and HiDES

Source 6

> The Rt Hon Arthur Henderson MP
>
> …In May 1915 the Party were unexpectedly invited by the late PM (Asquith) to associate with a new coalition government… The invitation was accepted and they had 18 months' experience. When he was sent for by the present PM he determined as far as possible, and with his colleagues when they waited on the PM at the war office also determined as far as they could to profit from the experience of the past 18 months.
>
> Mr J.R. Clynes (National Union of General Workers) said:
>
> He sympathised freely with the men who had accepted office in Labour's name. He looked forward 20 or more years to the period when the great labour movement could put these men in high offices of State…
>
> Finally, he believed, that in entering the government, Labour men had done the right thing as a matter of prosecuting the war to a successful issue and especially had done a just thing for the immediate claims of organised Labour.

Report of the 16th Annual Conference of the Labour Party
(January 1917), HiDES

THE TRIANGULAR TEST.

LIBERAL WHIP. "MY COW, I THINK."   LABOUR PARTY LEADER. "MY COW, I THINK."
UNIONIST CANDIDATE (*milking*). "MY CHANCE, ANYHOW."

Punch *cartoon 10 July 1912*

QUESTIONS ON THE SOURCES

1   In Source 5, what does the liberal Francis Hirst find unacceptable with the Liberal government's handling of the war?

2   In Source 6, what do Henderson and Clynes consider the Labour Party to have gained from the war?

TASK

After completing units 9 and 10 write an **essay** on how and why historians differ in their interpretations of the strength of the Liberal Party before 1914.

Challenging History Resource Pack. Text © Liz Petheram; Illustrations © Thomas Nelson & Sons Ltd; Photographs © as listed on page 2; sourced texts on p. 4. Published by Thomas Nelson & Sons Ltd 1999.